White, Donna R.,
1955-
Dancing with
dragons

D0742606

Dancing With Dragons

About *Dancing with Dragons:*

Ursula K. Le Guin began to draw attention in the late 1960s with the publication of *A Wizard of Earthsea* (1968) and *The Left Hand of Darkness* (1969). The former, a young adult fantasy, established Le Guin as America's foremost contemporary fantasist; the latter, a science fiction novel, embroiled her in a feminist controversy that continues to this day. Both books started Le Guin on the road to being one of the most award-winning writers in America.

The moral force and stylistic sophistication of Le Guin's work demand a critical response that reviewers and scholars have been quick to provide. Journals such as *Science-Fiction Studies* and *Extrapolation* have devoted entire issues to Le Guin's science fiction and fantasy. The past two decades have seen the publication of a dozen books and hundreds of articles about her work. As an academically trained critic in her own right, Le Guin has never shied from critical confrontation, but she prefers discussion to warfare. For thirty years, she has maintained a dialogue with her critics, exploring with them her changing views on feminism, environmentalism, and utopia. A writer of realistic fiction, historical fiction, science fiction, children's literature, fantasy, poetry, reviews, and critical essays, Le Guin challenges genre classifications and writes what she will.

Dancing with Dragons brings together for the first time the various strands of Le Guin criticism to show how the author's dialogue with the critics has informed and influenced her work and her own critical stance. Well-known literary critics such as Robert Scholes, Fredric Jameson, and Harold Bloom have declared Le Guin to be a major voice in American letters. This volume examines how that reputation developed.

Professor Donna R. White has written articles on British children's literature, on Welsh legends, and on Lewis Carroll.

Ursula K. Le Guin
Photo by Marian Wood Kolisch

DONNA R. WHITE

DANCING WITH DRAGONS

URSULA K. LE GUIN
AND THE CRITICS

CAMDEN HOUSE

First published 1999
Camden House
Drawer 2025
Columbia, SC 29202–2025 USA

Camden House is an imprint of Boydell & Brewer Inc.
PO Box 41026, Rochester, NY 14604–4126 USA
and of Boydell & Brewer Limited
PO Box 9, Woodbridge, Suffolk IP12 3DF, UK

ISBN: 1–57113–034–9

Library of Congress Cataloging-in-Publication Data

White, Donna R., 1955-
        Dancing with dragons : Ursula K. Le Guin and the critics / Donna
R. White.
        p.   cm. – (Studies in English and American literature,
linguistics, and culture. Literary criticism in perspective)
        Includes bibliographical references (p.   ) and index.
        ISBN 1-57113-034-9 (acid-free paper)
        1. Le Guin, Ursula K., 1929-   -- Criticism and interpretation-
-History. 2. Children's stories, American—History and Criticism-
-Theory, etc. 3. Science fiction, American – History and criticism-
-Theory, etc. 4. Women and literature – United States – History –20th
century. 5. Criticism – United States – History – 20th century.
I. Title. II. Series: Studies in·English and American literature,
linguistics, and culture (Unnumbered). Literary criticism in
perspective.
PS3562.E42Z985 1998
813'.54—dc21   98-35209
                                                                   CIP

This publication is printed on acid-free paper.
Printed in the United States of America

for Kim

Contents

Acknowledgments

THREE MAIN SOURCES OF INFORMATION made this book possible. Ursula K. Le Guin, the most gracious person on any planet, freely granted interviews, answered nosy questions, and allowed me access to her personal files. She cooperated willingly in this project, and I owe her boundless gratitude. Secondly, this work would never have been completed if Elizabeth Cummins Cogell had not already done most of the footwork by compiling a Le Guin bibliography. That gave me a head start in collecting all the reviews and articles on Le Guin. Finally, the Interlibrary Loan staff of the Clemson University library tackled the Herculean task of finding most of the material I needed, even when it existed only in obscure Australian science fiction fan magazines. When my Interlibrary Loan requests reached 90 a week, I feared the librarians would hire a hit man to take me out of circulation, but other than wide-eyed stares every time I entered their office, they expressed no attitude other than cheerful helpfulness. I am grateful for their restraint as well as their assistance.

I would like to thank Jim Hardin and Jim Walker of Camden House for their infinite patience and my editor, Ben Franklin, for being much more efficient with his time than I am. (Ben, I promise never again to use the words "towards" and "amongst.") Many other people solved problems for me while I was working on this book. Charles Sullivan III of East Carolina University gave me Ursula K. Le Guin's address and encouraged me to write to her. David Lenander of the University of Minnesota library system broadcast my cry for help when I needed to locate hard-to-find fantasy and science fiction material; Ruth Berman answered the call, found the missing items, photocopied them, and sent them to me almost at the rate I made Interlibrary Loan requests. My colleagues at Clemson University nagged and encouraged as necessary. I owe particular thanks to Frank Day for pushing me toward this topic; to the late Carol Ingalls Johnston for connecting me to Camden House; and to Pam Draper, librarian extraordinaire, who babied me through long library searches.

The many friends who supported and encouraged and put up with me for the entire length of this project include Margaret Meredith, Laura Zaidman, Anita Tarr, Barbara Zaczek, Sharon Jones, Cheryl Collier, Joni Hurley, Ruth and Paul Jeffries, De Nise Pellinen, Eleanor Webb Landman, Pat Price, Susan Hyman, Jill Keen, Sharmila Patel, and my long-suffering family. I hope my insistent babbling hasn't put any of them off

Landman, Pat Price, Susan Hyman, Jill Keen, Sharmila Patel, and my long-suffering family. I hope my insistent babbling hasn't put any of them off Le Guin for life. This book is dedicated to Lori Kim Smith Troboy, my chief badgerer, who nagged me long distance with great persistence; without her there would be no words on these pages.

A NEH matching grant from Clemson University enabled me to travel to Portland to interview Ursula K. Le Guin. The bulk of my research was supported by a summer fellowship at the Oregon Humanities Center on the University of Oregon campus, where a comfortable office, a state-of-the-art computer, and friendly colleagues made my work a joy.

Introduction

URSULA K. LE GUIN RANKS AMONG THE most respected contemporary American authors. Known primarily for her speculative fiction in novels such as *The Left Hand of Darkness* (1969), *The Lathe of Heaven* (1971), *The Dispossessed* (1974), and four books set in the fantasy world of Earthsea, she also writes realistic fiction, nonfiction, screenplays, librettos, poetry, and any other kind of writing that a new idea seems to call for, most of which is either published to critical acclaim or greeted with bemused silence. If a new book falls under the rubric of a recognized genre such as science fiction, the readers and critics of that genre pounce upon the book eagerly, but if the new work happens to be a collection of realistic short stories set on the Pacific coast, it has to find a completely different audience. Because of her range, Le Guin's work is difficult to classify — a fact in which the author delights. Publishers and booksellers like labels, but they are seldom sure what label to use for Le Guin. The Barnes and Noble bookstore in Greenville, South Carolina shelves her books in seven different sections: science fiction and fantasy, children's books, young adult, literature, poetry, literary criticism, and women's studies.

Despite this genre confusion, Le Guin has become a major voice in American letters. Her work has been the focus of entire sessions at the annual Modern Language Association conferences and at the meetings of its regional branches. Ten volumes of criticism, at least forty dissertations, and more than two hundred scholarly articles about Le Guin have been written. A new Le Guin book will be reviewed in the *New York Times Book Review* and the *Times Literary Supplement,* and the notices tend to be written by authors whose renown rivals Le Guin's own. She herself often writes reviews for the *New York Times* and the *Washington Post,* and she graciously fends off continual invitations to give commencement addresses, write introductions, edit anthologies, teach university classes, and appear at conferences. Writing workshops, however, have a higher priority in her schedule; she finds interaction with other writers, whether beginning or experienced, stimulating. Le Guin's literary awards are too numerous to list in a single paragraph, but they include the prestigious National Book Award, the Newbery Medal, the Hugo, and the Nebula.

Attaining such literary heights was not an overnight process. Born in Berkeley, California on October 21, 1929 (St. Ursula's Day), Le Guin has been writing for more than thirty years. Before she was twelve years old, she had written several fantasy and science fiction stories and had even submitted one of them to *Astounding*, which rejected it. In fact, she had written four novels and an unknown number of short stories and poems in the ten years before she first saw publication. But once she found a market to target — the science fiction magazines — her rise to eminence was relatively quick. After publishing eleven poems, eight short stories, and three science fiction novels between 1959 and 1967, she received sudden critical acclaim for two books: *A Wizard of Earthsea* (1968), an original fantasy for young adults, and *The Left Hand of Darkness* (1969), her fourth science fiction novel. Discussion of these two books continues to this day, with critics like Harold Bloom pronouncing them her masterpieces.

Because these novels address different audiences in different genres, the criticism has taken two divergent paths. Critics of children's literature have claimed possession of *A Wizard of Earthsea* and its three sequels, while the science fiction community has a lien on *The Left Hand of Darkness* and all other works set in Le Guin's fictional future universe. As a result of this divergence and of Le Guin's later work in other genres, criticism of Le Guin has become balkanized. Most science fiction scholars remain unaware of criticism in the field of children's literature, for example. Critics who publish in mainstream literary journals often have no idea there is a large body of criticism available in the marginalized genres of science fiction and children's literature.

Le Guin also writes poetry, picture books, reviews, scholarly articles, personal essays, travel pieces, speeches, short stories, letters, chapbooks, and anthologies. Of these, the essays and articles have attracted the most critical attention, partly because they engage the author in the critical debate over her work in particular and the fields of science fiction and fantasy in general, partly because Le Guin has the good sense to gather miscellaneous pieces into more accessible single volumes, and partly because scholarship that addresses the other genres is sparse. Picture books and anthologies are often reviewed but seldom become the subject of scholarly articles. Modern poetry has a small audience of practitioners and teachers, and travel writing is generally ignored by critics. Literary criticism is stratified and hierarchical. Science fiction commentators may revile "the literary establishment," but they are well aware that a review in the *New York Times* is worth any number of reviews in science fiction magazines. Literary scholars know that an article in *PMLA* will boost their careers more readily than a piece in *Mythlore*. In the hierarchy of criticism, realistic fiction holds center stage and progresses through various critical fads: Marxism, feminism, deconstruction, queer studies, and so on. Criticism of genres other than realistic fiction must struggle for recognition and acceptance, yet critics of marginalized genres like science fiction and children's literature often exhibit the same hierarchical values as the mainstream critics. Thus, science fiction critics look down on children's literature as beneath notice and children's literature critics behave as if young adult literature does not exist. Literary criticism is, above all else, territorial. Critics in various fields have carved out large and small chunks of Le Guin's work to mark as their territory while ignoring the rest of her work and those who discuss it. Le Guin may be the only critic who is aware of the full extent of her work, and that awareness, coupled with a sharp intellect that can disengage itself from the role of author, makes Le Guin herself the most astute of her critics.

Le Guin entered the scholarly lists with full academic credentials: not only was she raised in a university setting, but she also has a master's degree in Romance Language and Literature from Columbia University and completed most of the work for a Ph.D. at that same institution. Her father, noted anthropologist Alfred Kroeber, taught at Berkeley and filled his house with intelligent and accomplished visitors from all walks of life. Theodora Kroeber, Le Guin's mother, became a well-known writer of children's books and biographies. Le Guin married into academia, too — her husband is historian Charles Le Guin — and raised her three children in academic surroundings. Her brother Karl is an English professor at Columbia University, and her two other brothers are a professional psychologist and a historian. This close proximity to the world of learning equipped her to respond fully and in kind to critical commentary on her work. In fact, she played a role in bringing science fiction and fantasy into critical respectability by supporting the formation of scholarly organizations and journals devoted to the study of those fields. She serves on editorial boards for academic journals such as *Paradoxa* and *Science-Fiction Studies*, and supports the work of the International Association of the Fantastic in the Arts and the Science Fiction Research Association. She regularly associates herself with scholars at conferences and workshops, and she occasionally takes on the role of writer-in-residence at major universities. Le Guin also maintains correspondence with scholars of her work and cooperates in the critical process in every way she can.

Because of her close connection with scholars and critics, criticism of Le Guin's earlier work has strongly influenced her later work. Feminist criticism in particular has affected Le Guin's style and subject matter. A sharp feminist response to *The Left Hand of Darkness* led Le Guin to question her own attitudes and opinions and resulted in a change of heart and political orientation. She began to experiment with structure and language and point of view, and the resultant works stimulated further critical dialogue. Because the critical dialogue has been so influential on her work, a knowledge of the criticism is vital to an understanding of Le Guin and her place in American literature.

The dialogue between Le Guin and her critics has been angry, congratulatory, accusatory, defensive, celebratory, and downright rude. Science fiction writer Norman Spinrad's 1986 attack on Le Guin's *Always Coming Home* in *Isaac Asimov's Science Fiction Magazine* accused Le Guin of selling out to mainstream literature, referring to her as a "token nigger" of the literary establishment, a "noble granola-eating natural woman," and a "hectoring guru." Le Guin responded to this attack with humor and grace in a public letter to the editor which she signed "Granola Eating Woman." But despite her best efforts to practice the Taoist principle of non-aggression, on rare occasions Le Guin's anger gets the best of her and she responds to accusations with a heated defense of her work. When the *Times Literary Supplement* published a less than laudatory review of *Tehanu: The Last Book of Earthsea*, Le Guin wrote and published in chapbook form an essay entitled *Earthsea Revisioned* that defended her feminist change of perspective in the eighteen years since writing the first three books about Earthsea. Le Guin freely admits the essay was written in angry response to negative reviews of the book, but it is a controlled anger that refrains from personal attack.

Maintaining a dialogue with critics is a daunting task for an author. Like the "flame wars" that occur on computer discussion lists, the discussion between critic and author can easily become inflammatory. An author has to muster great patience, fortitude, and stamina to endure criticism of work that is intensely personal. One critical barb can sting so sharply that no amount of praise can heal the wound. Since creative writers are often isolated, introverted individualists with skin little thicker than tissue paper, only a rare person is capable of engaging honestly in the critical debate over her work. But Le Guin is a rarity. To put it in terms of one of the author's own fantasy images, she is a person who interacts with dragons. Like the dragonlords in her Earthsea books, she is "one whom the dragons will speak with," and like her heroine Tenar in *Tehanu*, she is a woman who will look the dragons in the eye and speak to them in their own language. As the wizard Ged explains, "The question is always the same, with a dragon: will he talk with you or will he eat you?" (*Tombs of Atuan* 95). Critics can gobble up an author with one or two negative reviews in influential publications, but Le Guin refuses to be eaten. Her dialogue with the critics falls into clear patterns, rather like a dance. The critic bows and steps forward, Le Guin steps back, then they twirl once around the topic, occasionally stepping on each other's toes. Le Guin seizes the lead and starts executing her own dance. In an essay entitled "A

Non-Euclidean View of California as a Cold Place to Be," she refers to a Native American song called "Dancing at the edge of the world" — an apt metaphor for her interaction with the dragon-critics.

The purpose of this volume is to examine the steps of that dance. Like other books in the series *Literary Criticism in Perspective*, this study traces the literary scholarship and criticism about a major writer as a means to explore the interdependence of creative writing and scholarship and to show the influence of social and historic currents on aesthetic judgments. Books in the series address a readership of scholars and students and interested bystanders. One of the goals of the series is to illuminate the nature of literary criticism itself. Part of that nature is dragonish: powerful, potentially destructive, yet able to soar on wings of praise.

This volume will take a generally chronological view of the critical reception of Le Guin's works. However, the balkanized nature of Le Guin scholarship requires a modified arrangement. Chapter One deals with the first three books of the Earthsea series: *A Wizard of Earthsea* (1968), *The Tombs of Atuan* (1970), and *The Farthest Shore* (1972). For eighteen years these young adult fantasies were considered a trilogy and were discussed as such by critics. Although Le Guin published three science fiction novels prior to this, they received no critical attention, being reviewed only briefly in science fiction magazines little known outside the field. The Earthsea books were the first of Le Guin's works to attract the attention of a major critic — the children's writer Eleanor Cameron, who wrote an insightful article in 1971 — and to gather a substantial body of criticism. Although criticism of *The Left Hand of Darkness* began upon its publication in 1969, the first major critical voice to address Le Guin's science fiction was that of Robert Scholes in 1974.

Chapter Two, therefore, backtracks to 1969 to deal with Le Guin's early science fiction leading up to and including *The Left Hand of Darkness*, which was the center of a heated feminist debate in the science fiction community. After Scholes acclaimed the book publicly, critical commentary multiplied exponentially. Chapter Three deals with Le Guin's forays into utopian literature, primarily *The Dispossessed* and *Always Coming Home*. In Chapter Four a miscellany of books for children and young adults as well as Le Guin's poetry and her realistic fiction about the imagined country Orsinia share the spotlight. Chapter Four also looks at Le Guin's more recent work, starting with *Buffalo Gals and Other Animal Presences* in 1988 and paying particular attention to *Tehanu: The Last Book of Earthsea*, which gave rise to another feminist — or rather, anti-feminist — controversy. This final chapter also summarizes and evaluates the development of critical commentary on Le Guin in order to connect the divergent critical channels.

Earlier attempts to evaluate Le Guin criticism have been invaluable to this study. The first such overview is found in Joe De Bolt's 1979 collection of critical articles, *Ursula K. Le Guin: Voyager to Inner Lands and to Outer Space*. De Bolt included "A Survey of Le Guin Criticism" by James W. Bittner, which traces the early criticism. Elizabeth Cummins Cogell's excellent bibliography of Le Guin contains a brief essay summarizing the criticism up to 1981. Published by G. K. Hall in 1983, Cogell's *Ursula K. Le Guin: A Primary and Secondary Bibliography* is a primer for Le Guin scholars. Margaret P. Esmonde's essay "The Good Witch of the West," published in the annual *Children's Literature* in 1981, also summarizes Le Guin criticism, which blossomed in the late 1970s. Although there are half a dozen primary bibliographies of Le Guin's work, David S. Bratman's unpublished 1995 compilation is the most useful and complete, but it is only available from the author. Secondary bibliographies are harder to come by. Cogell's thorough listing of secondary sources has not yet been duplicated or updated. Since Le Guin and her critics have continued to write after 1981, eighteen years of scholarship lie unexamined.

Works Cited

Bittner, James W. "A Survey of Le Guin Criticism." *Ursula K. Le Guin: Voyager to Inner Lands and to Outer Space*. Ed. Joe De Bolt. Literary Criticism Series. Port Washington, NY: Kennikat Press, 1979. 31–49.

Bratman, David S. Ursula K. Le Guin: A Primary Bibliography. Unpublished, 1995.

Cameron, Eleanor. "High Fantasy: *A Wizard of Earthsea*." *Crosscurrents of Criticism: Horn Book Essays 1968–1977*. Ed. Paul Heins. Boston: Horn Book, 1977. 333–41.

Clute, John. "Deconstructing Paradise." Rev. of *Tehanu*. *Times Literary Supplement* 28 December 1990: 1409.

Cogell, Elizabeth Cummins. *Ursula K. Le Guin: A Primary and Secondary Bibliography*. Boston: G. K. Hall, 1983.

Esmonde, Margaret P. "The Good Witch of the West." *Children's Literature* 9 (1981): 185–90.

Le Guin, Ursula K. *Always Coming Home*. New York: Harper & Row, 1985.

——. *Buffalo Gals and Other Animal Presences*. Santa Barbara: Capra Press, 1987.

——. *The Dispossessed*. New York: Harper & Row, 1974.

——. *Earthsea Revisioned*. Cambridge: Green Bay Publications, 1993.

——. *The Farthest Shore*. New York: Atheneum, 1972.

——. *The Lathe of Heaven.* New York: Scribner's, 1971.

——. *The Left Hand of Darkness.* New York: Ace, 1969.

——. Letter to the editor. *Isaac Asimov's Science Fiction Magazine* (April 1987): 14.

——. "A Non-Euclidean View of California as a Cold Place to Be." *Dancing at the Edge of the World.* New York: Harper & Row, 1989. 80–100.

——. *Tehanu: The Last Book of Earthsea.* New York: Atheneum, 1990.

——. *The Tombs of Atuan.* New York: Atheneum, 1971.

——. *A Wizard of Earthsea.* Berkeley: Parnassus Press, 1968.

Scholes, Robert. "The Good Witch of the West." *Hollins Critic* 11 (April 1974): 1–12.

Spinrad, Norman. "Critical Standards." *Isaac Asimov's Science Fiction Magazine* (September 1986). *Science Fiction in the Real World.* Carbondale: Southern Illinois UP, 1990. 3–17.

1: Earthsea

URSULA LE GUIN NEVER SET OUT TO BE A children's writer, even though she had a role model in her mother, Theodora Kroeber. In graduate school, her interest was French Renaissance poetry, and her first — and long unpublished — fiction was set in the imaginary European country of Orsinia, which shared the history of the rest of continental Europe. Between 1959 and 1961 Le Guin's early poetry and one Orsinian story found a limited market in small literary magazines and journals, but most of her fiction remained homeless until she decided to try writing science fiction and fantasy. Her voracious childhood reading had included science fiction, mainly stories in pulp magazines such as *Thrilling Wonder* and *Astounding*, so the field was not entirely new to her. Moreover, the science fiction magazines actually paid writers for their work — not much, to be sure, but the only remuneration in the literary journals was the pleasure of seeing one's name in print. Between 1962 and 1965 Le Guin sold seven stories to *Fantastic* and *Amazing*, two of the magazines that catered to readers of science fiction and fantasy. Following this small success, she quickly wrote and sold three science fiction novels to Ace.

Le Guin's entrance into literature for younger readers came about because of a family connection, cultural developments, and her own modest publication history. In 1967 Herman Schein of Parnassus Press asked Le Guin to write an original novel for young adults. Young adults — an indeterminate age group teetering somewhere between childhood and adulthood — constituted a newly recognized publishing market. S. E. Hinton's *The Outsiders*, a story about a close-knit group of sensitive teens who belong to an inner city gang, was published in 1967 and became a huge success. Its popularity stirred up much discussion about literature for teenagers. The arguments Hinton raised in an article for the *New York Times Book Review* were that teenagers had concerns and problems very different from those of children and that they therefore needed a literature that addressed the differences. Since Hinton was herself a teenager, she seemed to speak with authority. More compelling to publishers were the sales figures for *The Outsiders*. Parnassus Press was only one of many that wished to tap into this new market. Parnassus already published books for children, including works by Le Guin's mother. Theodora Kroeber's most notable book for children, *Ishi, Last of His Tribe*, was a Parnassus publication.

Although Le Guin had never written anything for young people, she kept an open mind about all kinds of literature. She was also aware that science fiction is a genre popular with teenagers, so writing specifically for that age group might not be a huge stretch. When Schein asked her to write a book for teens, Le Guin was flattered — nobody had ever sought her out as a writer. There was also the family connection through her mother. So Le Guin agreed to attempt it.

With no background in children's literature and no preconceptions about the limitations of young adult readers, Le Guin proceeded with the project much as she would for any other work. She had recently published two short stories about a fantasy land where wizards and dragons dueled, and as she pondered over what to write, these stories came to mind. Fantasy had long been a staple of children's literature, but the American educational establishment had turned against it in the wake of Sputnik, favoring math and science over imaginative and speculative reading. Whether or not Le Guin was aware of it, American fantasy for children was enjoying a renaissance in the 1960s, primarily because of the publication of the first three volumes of Lloyd Alexander's award-winning Chronicles of Prydain, so her choice of genre was serendipitous. When he began his fantasy series in 1964, Alexander faced resistance from publishers, librarians and educators who castigated fantasy as mere escapism, but the wide acceptance of his children's fantasies and the dramatic publicity and success surrounding the first American paperback editions of J. R. R. Tolkien's immense adult fantasy *The Lord of the Rings* in 1965 gave fantasy a new cachet. Le Guin chose an opportune moment to enter the field.

The two fantasy stories Le Guin had already published were "The Word of Unbinding" and "The Rule of Names." The former had appeared in the January 1964 issue of *Fantastic*. The story concerned a good wizard's struggle to free himself and his land from the power of an evil wizard. This tale later provided the plot for Le Guin's third Earthsea book, *The Farthest Shore*. In April of the same year *Fantastic* published "The Rule of Names," a more humorous story set in the same world that dealt with a duel over treasure between a wizard and a dragon. The setting for these two stories is an archipelago, a group of islands where talented individuals can learn to control great magical powers. This place gripped Le Guin's imagination, so she wished to explore it further.

Contemplating a readership of young people on the verge of adulthood, Le Guin decided that the theme of coming-of-age would be appropriate for her first venture into young adult literature. The book that resulted was *A Wizard of Earthsea*, the story of the youthful exploits of the wizard Ged, who was destined to become the greatest mage of the land. Le Guin drew on her extensive knowledge of myth and legend as well as the anthropological interests that had surrounded her from baby-hood to produce a work of such depth and originality that critics were bound to take notice. She created entire cultures for the islands of the ar-chipelago as well as a physics based on the ecological balance of magic and nature.

A Wizard of Earthsea recounts Ged's early experiments with magic; his initial training under the tutelage of an aunt; the spell that saves his village from invaders and draws the attention of one of Earthsea's greatest mages, who continues the boy's training and later sends him to a famous school for wizards; and most importantly, the youthful arrogance and pride that lead Ged to use a spell he cannot control and thus loose a powerful and shapeless shadow that threatens the magical balance of Earthsea. Ged's pursuit of the shadow, and its pursuit of him, take up the final three-fourths of the book. The pursuit takes Ged and the reader from island to island, providing a glimpse into the rich multiplicity of cultures and socie-ties in Earthsea.

Despite a few mixed reviews, initial response to the book was positive. Ruth H. Viguers in *Horn Book Magazine* and Elva Harmon in *Library Journal* (two influential review organs for children's literature) praised it highly, and the American Library Association placed it on several of their "Best Books" lists. Since librarians were the arbiters of fashion for chil-dren's books and young adult literature was subsumed under that cate-gory, their acceptance of the book was vital to its reception and sales. In 1969 the book won the *Boston Globe-Horn Book* Award for Excellence — a children's book award second only to the Newbery Medal in prestige and importance — and this despite the fact that Parnassus Press was not a major player in the field of children's publishing and therefore its publica-tions did not automatically draw the kind of critical attention that usually leads to notable awards. The book fared equally well when it came out in Britain in 1971, where Naomi Lewis, the reviewer for the *Times Literary Supplement*, selected it as the best book of the year for young readers. The English have traditionally valued children's fantasy more highly than have Americans, so the enthusiastic reception of the work in Britain lacked the note of grudging admiration that sounds in the background of American reviews of fantasy literature. In fact, British teachers quickly adopted the book for classroom use, and two articles about teaching it (one by Wendy Jago and the other by Geoff Fox) came out in Britain's leading children's literature journal, *Children's Literature in Education*, within two years of its British publication.

The first serious critical analysis of Le Guin's work came in 1969 when noted children's writer and critic Eleanor Cameron delivered a talk to the New England Round Table of Children's Librarians. The talk, entitled

"High Fantasy: *A Wizard of Earthsea*," was reprinted in *Horn Book Maga-zine* in 1971 and included in a collection of notable *Horn Book* essays in 1977. High fantasy, set in a magical and pre-industrial Otherworld where great-hearted heroes perform noble deeds in epic struggles between good and evil, was the subject of the the 1969 Round Table. The choice of topic reflected the recent change in attitude toward fantasy among librari-ans. However, the change was so recent that supporters of fantasy, and fantasy writers in particular, still tended to be defensive on the subject. Cameron therefore adopts a defensive tone at the beginning of her talk, selecting *A Wizard of Earthsea* as an exemplum of high fantasy and showing the depth and seriousness of both the genre and this particular example of it.

Cameron's discussion is peppered with personal tidbits about Le Guin, not surprisingly, since the two writers corresponded about fantasy and lit-erature. However, Cameron approaches the novel as a writer and a reader rather than as a friend, and her comments on the work are perceptive and thoughtful. She mentions Le Guin's family background in anthropology and shows its influence on the highly detailed picture of life in the archi-pelago of Earthsea. According to Cameron, anthropology manifests itself as a mood and an attitude rather than as a science. This is the same atti-tude that informs Le Guin's science fiction books, although Cameron admits to less enjoyment of these than of Le Guin's fantasy. Science fic-tion critics would later make the same "discovery" about the influence of anthropology on Le Guin's work, but Cameron's talk is the first instance of recognition. Cameron is also the first of many critics to point out that Le Guin's shadow bears a close resemblance to the Jungian archetype of the same name and that Ged's final struggle with the shadow reflects Jung's concept of individuation. The names Le Guin uses in Earthsea strike Cameron with particular intensity, and she links the importance of names and shadows in Earthsea to Sir James Frazer's *The Golden Bough*. Cameron praises *Wizard* as a work of high fantasy that has the virtue of wholeness through its wealth of persuasive detail:

> To me, it is as if Ursula Le Guin herself has lived on the Archipelago, mi-
> nutely observing and noting down the habits and idiosyncracies [*sic*] of
> the culture from island to island, variations in dress and food and ways of
> living, in climate, languages, attitudes of the inhabitants and atmospheres
> of cities and towns. Nothing has escaped the notice of her imagination's
> seeking eye, but always she has chosen her details with the discrimination
> of an artist for whom economy of style is the ideal. (340)

Since Cameron was a respected writer and critic, librarians listened to her. So did critics of children's literature, although scholarly criticism of the field as literature was still in its infancy. Children's literature — and by extension young adult literature — received attention from educators and librarians, who had taken it seriously since the seventeenth century and had contributed a wealth of insight into the educational merits of children's books as well as their role in cognition and reading development. However, in the 1960s literary scholars were just beginning to apply the tools of literary theory to the genre, in the face of general disapproval from their English departments and occasional territorial disputes with librarians and teachers. Anyone who wanted a Ph.D. with a specialization in children's literature had to apply to schools of library science or education, so the emerging literary scholars were often self-taught. Since science fiction studies were in a similar stage of development, early Le Guin criticism was not as rigorous and informed as criticism of the major literary figures of realistic adult fiction. Cameron's article stands out among the first critical responses to Le Guin, and Cameron's reputation brought attention and acceptance to the younger author — at least among the people who studied children's literature.

No further important scholarly work appeared on Le Guin until after the publication of the next two Earthsea books. The second book in the series, *The Tombs of Atuan*, appeared in 1971. It was the full-length version of a long story by the same title that had been published in the first volume of *Worlds of Fantasy* in an issue dated 1970–1971. Le Guin had cut the novel for magazine publication. The expanded novel was published by Atheneum, a highly respected name in children's publishing. Soon after the publication of *A Wizard of Earthsea*, Le Guin had found a literary agent, Virginia Kidd, who objected to the terms of the Parnassus contract and arranged a more remunerative deal with Atheneum. Kidd's aggressive and knowledgeable representation would place Le Guin's work in excellent markets for the next thirty years, and the two would form a close, collaborative friendship to their mutual benefit.

The Tombs of Atuan tells the story of Tenar, a priestess of unnamed gods on a brutal and militaristic island far from Ged's home island. Tenar lives in a world of women, though isolated from them by her position as high priestess. She alone has access to the dark labyrinth below the temple — the abode of the gods she serves. The first part of the book tells of Tenar's life in this oppressive environment, but the real action begins when the teen-aged Tenar finds Ged in her labyrinth and imprisons him there. Ged is now at the height of his powers, but even wizardry cannot help him escape from the labyrinth without help. He has come in search of the lost half of a ring that when whole will form the Bond-Rune, the sign of dominion and peace that will restore the lost kingship of Earthsea. Ged forges a tentative relationship with Tenar, and eventually she decides to help him escape with the ring. Her decision comes at the cost of great personal sacrifice, but she too regains her freedom and a new life.

Although *The Tombs of Atuan* garnered no in-depth written criticism, the majority of the reviews glowed with praise for the author's storytelling skills and her grasp of the mythic. Science fiction writer Ted White, reviewing the book in *Fantastic Science Fiction*, found the book incomplete and unconvincing, and Jennifer Farley Smith complained in the *Christian Science Monitor* that the novel was permeated with a sense of desolation and a nightmarish atmosphere; however, these two negative voices were in the minority. In Britain, the book was reviewed by no less a personage than John Rowe Townsend, a children's writer and critic of immense literary clout. Some reviewers saw the story as allegorical and others perceived a retelling of the Ariadne myth. The book was nominated for both the Newbery Medal and the National Book Award. Although it won neither, it was named a Newbery Honor Book — high praise from the American Library Association. *The Tombs of Atuan* was in excellent company that year. The Newbery Medalist was Robert C. O'Brien's *Mrs. Frisby and the Rats of NIMH*, an animal fantasy that explored the consequences of scientific experimentation. One of the other Honor Books was Virginia Hamilton's *The Planet of Junior Brown*. Both of these novels have proved to be modern classics for children, as have the first three books about Earthsea. (Because *Tehanu: The Last Book of Earthsea* was published in 1990, it is too soon to tell if it will join this elite company.) Reviewers of *The Tombs of Atuan* expressed a wish for a further volume about Earthsea, and Le Guin did not disappoint them.

The Farthest Shore, the conclusion of the trilogy, appeared in 1972. The story takes place toward the end of Ged's career as a wizard. After a lifetime of exploits, he is now the Archmage of Earthsea, the highest wizard in the land. When he receives news of magic gone awry in the far reaches of the archipelago, he sets out on a journey with young prince Arren to find the source of the disturbance and end it. Their journey takes them to many islands, and on all of them the failure of faith and magic is leading to despair and self-destruction. With Arren's assistance, Ged tracks the problem to the Land of the Dead, where the wizard Cob, because of his own fear of dying, has created an opening between life and death that is disrupting both. At the cost of his wizardly power, Ged closes the breach and restores balance to Earthsea. Because Ged is nearly destroyed by his efforts, Arren must single-handedly find a way back to living lands for himself and the older man. This arduous journey forms Arren into the king promised by prophecy, as Ged has recognized from the first. Arren is crowned king of all Earthsea, and Ged disappears on dragonback never to be seen again (or so readers must conclude until *Tehanu*).

The reception of this third book of Earthsea was even more enthusiastic than that of the previous volumes. Here was an author dealing with one of the ultimate themes of life — death — in a new way, and with complete candor. Neither Arren nor Ged is heroic in the usual sense; Ged is often tired and confused, and Arren's own fear of death controls him for most of the book. The Land of the Dead is not a beautiful, happy Otherworld, but rather a wasteland populated by emotionless ghosts that owes more to the classical Hades and to T. S. Eliot than to the Christian concept of Heaven. Yet Le Guin's characters find hope in the midst of dark despair, and personal sacrifice brings a promise of peace for all of Earthsea.

Reviewers embraced the book, except for Karen Rappaport in the *Science Fiction Review Monthly*, who found it a disappointment, objecting to its slow pace and the lack of female characters. Peter Nicholls, reviewing the book for the British science fiction journal *Foundation*, claimed that Le Guin was a better fantasy writer than the English master of fantasy, J. R. R. Tolkien — that, in fact, she is on a par with Dante. Like the previous volume about Earthsea, *The Farthest Shore* was nominated for the National Book Award, and this second nomination proved successful. "National Book Award" sounds prestigious, and indeed the publishers who founded the prize intended it to be prestigious. As far as the adult categories are concerned, the National Book Award is the next best thing to a Pulitzer; however, the children's literature award never became the supreme accolade envisioned when it was established. The awards were started in 1950, but a category for children's literature was not instituted until 1969. The award in this category had a short life, lasting only until 1983. The 1973 awards generated disagreement over three of the ten categories. The judges came to split decisions in two categories, but in children's literature *The Farthest Shore* was the unanimous choice of the three judges. The disagreement in this case was over whether the category should continue. There were, after all, other awards for children's literature that received more recognition and the National Book Committee had recently lost much of its funding from the Association of American Publishers — a dire blow for an organization that gives cash prizes. This argument resurfaced many times in the next ten years before the National Book Committee finally dropped the children's literature category. Even then the argument did not die; the committee continued to argue over having children's awards until 1996, when the category was finally reinstated.

With the "Earthsea trilogy" now complete, critics began to discuss the series as a whole. The first important commentary came from the author herself. Ever since the first book won the *Boston Globe-Horn Book* Award, Le Guin had been an invited speaker at numerous gatherings of librarians, writers, and science fiction enthusiasts. She prepared for these occasions with diligence and thoughtfulness, and the resultant speeches were eventually published in a volume of literary criticism called *The Language of the Night* (1979), edited by Susan Wood. Most of the speeches deal with fantasy and science fiction, sometimes defending them, sometimes explaining them, sometimes analyzing them. Le Guin approaches her chosen genres with scholarly rigor, giving them the serious literary consideration she considered necessary for their continued health. One of the articles in this collection is "Dreams Must Explain Themselves," which was written in 1973 for the science fiction magazine *Algol*. In response to the editor's request for something about herself, Le Guin wrote an essay about the creation of Earthsea.

As she recounts in this essay, Le Guin did not plan Earthsea, but rather discovered it bit by bit in her unconscious mind. She explored the islands one by one and came to know the characters as human beings. In fact, Ged was so forceful a character that he wrested control from the author in *The Farthest Shore*. Le Guin mentions the importance of Taoist philosophy to her personal world view and points out her tendency to structure novels as spiral journeys. Both of these insights have provided paths for later critics to explore. However, Le Guin's most telling comments are about the themes of the Earthsea books:

> The trilogy is, in one aspect, about the artist. The artist as magician. The Trickster. Prospero. That is the only truly allegorical aspect it has of which I am conscious . . . . Wizardry is artistry. The trilogy is then, in this sense, about art, the creative experience, the creative process.
>
> (*Language* 53)

She later mentions more specific themes for each book: *A Wizard of Earthsea* is about coming-of-age, *The Tombs of Atuan* is about sex, and *The Farthest Shore* is about death. By sex she means not only sexuality, which shows itself in symbols she did not consciously recognize while writing, but also a female coming-of-age. Tenar's process of growth differs from Ged's because of her gender. "Dreams Must Explain Themselves" became a much-quoted reference for Le Guin scholars, as indeed did most of the essays in *The Language of the Night*. Not only did these articles give insight into the creative mind, but they also contributed high level literary criticism in two genres where quality criticism was yet a rare phenomenon.

Several of Le Guin's other early essays comment indirectly on Earthsea. "Why Are Americans Afraid of Dragons?" is an article that originated as a talk at the 1973 Pacific Northwest Library Association in Portland. In this essay Le Guin explores the American disapproval of fantasy as escapism and defends imagination as "one of the most deeply human, and humane" of human faculties, arguing that something can be "true" without having to be "real" (*Language* 44). The article is clearly intended as a defense of her own fantasy books for young people.

"The Child and the Shadow," which began as a lecture at the Library of Congress in celebration of Children's Book Week in 1974, presents Le Guin's interpretation of Carl Jung's concept of archetype. She is particularly concerned with the Shadow archetype, which represents an individual's repressed self — the primitive, undeveloped, negative, creative, dark, animalistic part of a person. This is not to say that the Shadow is evil: integration of the Shadow is an absolute necessity for wholeness of personality. The Shadow is also the guide to the deeper reaches of the unconscious, where lie the wellsprings of creation, and that journey into the unconscious is what true fantasy is about. Le Guin's comments on the Shadow have a clear connection to the shadow in *A Wizard of Earthsea*, even though she has elsewhere said that she had not read Jung at the time of its writing. She believes she independently discovered the same truth Jung had taught. Rather than conquering or destroying his own shadow beast, Ged integrates it by calling it by his own name and uniting with it to make himself whole. This closely resembles the process Jung termed individuation.

Le Guin's literary criticism proved to be influential. Her most quoted article, "From Elfland to Poughkeepsie," was responsible for renewing an interest in the work of a long-forgotten fantasy author, Kenneth Morris. She published this examination of fantasy style as a chapbook in 1973. She lists Morris with J. R. R. Tolkien as a master stylist. Because of her comments, readers sought out Morris's work, long out of print, and eventually Morris's posthumous fantasy novel and a collection of short stories were published. The same article contained negative comments about an unnamed modern fantasist whom knowledgeable readers had no difficulty identifying as Katherine Kurtz. This is a rare instance of personal criticism; in the future Le Guin would take great pains not to single out any individual living writer for negative remarks. In fact, in her book reviews she cushions negative criticism to such an extent that a careless reader sometimes misinterprets criticism as praise. If she had known how influential her comments would be, especially when published in *The Language of the Night*, she probably would not have written such pointed criticism of a fellow fantasy writer.

All of these talks and essays expressed the ideas Le Guin held in the early 1970s, before she immersed herself in feminist theory and radicalized her perception of both fantasy and science fiction. Le Guin was the only important critic examining her fantasy novels in the first part of the decade, although reviews of her books were popping up everywhere. An article by Douglas Barbour that was scarcely noticed outside of science fiction circles appeared in the *Riverside Quarterly* in 1974; it is notable for being the first exploration of Taoist themes in *Wizard*. The following year the University of Notre Dame Press published Robert Scholes's *Structural Fabulation*, based on lectures the eminent critic had given at Notre Dame. Scholes's main intent was to dignify science fiction as a literary form, but his fourth lecture, which focuses on Le Guin as an exemplum of all that is literary about science fiction, includes commentary on the Earthsea trilogy. This section is a revised version of an article on Le Guin published in *Hollins Critic* in 1974. Scholes is widely credited with initiating the serious literary criticism of Le Guin's work. Such attention from a major critic stimulated science fiction scholars to look more closely at the fantasies. Meanwhile, teachers began to churn out simple articles on how to teach *Wizard*, and librarians added all three novels to lists of recommended books for children and young adults.

Criticism of Le Guin's work blossomed in the late seventies. Most of the criticism addressed her science fiction exclusively, but several insightful analyses of the Earthsea trilogy appeared before the end of the decade. The first assessment of the trilogy as a whole was a chapter in George Slusser's *The Farthest Shores of Ursula K. Le Guin*, published by Borgo Press in 1976. This was the third volume of the series Popular Writers of Today. Le Guin's inclusion so early in the series was an indication of her growing reputation. Although Slusser's main interest is in her science fiction, he devotes fifteen pages to the three books about Earthsea.

The main thesis of Slusser's slim book is that Le Guin's work is a consistent whole rather than a process of evolution, so he seeks to make connections among all her books. Following Barbour's lead, Slusser sees Taoism as the unifying force behind her work; this philosophy is responsible for her concern with the balance of opposites. Slusser views the three books of Earthsea as an optimistic counterbalance to the pessimistic science fiction Le Guin was writing during the same period, 1968–1974. Ged is a new kind of hero for Le Guin — the artist-magician whose actions can influence the world. Despite his magical powers, he wins his most important victories through normal human means. All three books deal with the nature of evil, but it is a non-Christian perspective on evil. Evil is simply "a misunderstanding of the dynamics of life" (35).

According to Slusser, Ged is like the sorcerer's apprentice — he acts before he has the wisdom or knowledge to understand what he is doing. The shadow beast he releases in Earthsea is his own fear of mortality; it is a dangerously powerful shadow because Ged himself is such a powerful wizard. Ged must learn the hard way that actions have consequences and that he is responsible for his individual actions. As Slusser puts it, "The hardest task for Ged is not the heroic deed; it is the act of mind which necessarily denies his exceptional nature, and places him on a level with all the rest — the acceptance of his common mortality" (37). The evil is not death itself, but rather Ged's denial of its part in the balance of life. The true battle occurs not in a physical place but in Ged's mind.

Slusser is one of the few critics to give serious attention to *The Tombs of Atuan*. He sees Ged's search for the lost ring of Erreth-Akbe as his true public act, whereas his actions in the first book were private ones. The lost ring will restore peace and harmony to Earthsea, where for many years a false imposed unity has ruled. On this point Slusser seems to misinterpret the novel, for Le Guin's point is that there is no unity at all among the islands — just scattered strongholds of soldiers, priests, or wizards. However, Slusser is correct in saying that true harmony results only from "the gift freely given" (39). The first half of the broken ring came to Ged as a gift from a half-wild woman in *A Wizard of Earthsea*. The second half must come freely, too, from Tenar the priestess. Ged does not realize this truth at first or he would not have attempted to break into the labyrinth to steal the ring. But he learns quickly that the most his powers can do is to keep the darkness at bay; only Tenar can give him the ring and his freedom. In turn, he gives her back her true name and a chance for a new life. Tenar is reborn when Ged gives her back the name that was taken from her in childhood, but rebirth is a heavy burden. Slusser sees light and darkness as important images in the book. The light is associated with Ged and with the joining of opposites. The reverse image, according to Slusser, is of a self-sufficient spider "weaving his futile web out of himself in dry, dark places" (41).

Slusser points out that the image of the spider recurs in *The Farthest Shore*. The villain is a wizard named Cob, which means spider, and Le Guin uses many spider images throughout the book. Cob is also, in a sense, Ged's shadow self, in that Ged is indirectly responsible for Cob's fear of death and determination to surmount it. Many years earlier, in an effort to punish Cob for his irresponsible use of power over the dead, Ged had dragged Cob to the wall which separates the living lands from the land of the dead and forced him to look at the reality of death. Presenting Cob as Ged's doppelgänger rounds out the trilogy by bringing it back to the struggle against the shadow in the first volume. To Slusser, *The Farthest Shore* is a work of "genuine epic vision" (34). Of the three volumes in the trilogy, this novel holds his deepest admiration.

Slusser states that the view of life changes in *The Farthest Shore*. In the two earlier books there was a basic faith in the ultimate balance of life, but in this novel the system of checks and balances seems to be failing. Magic is failing; men and dragons are going mad; everyone is afraid of death.

Although the action apparently takes place in the external world, the real struggle is inward. To Slusser, this makes the book an allegory. Indeed, he sees all three books as allegorical in this way, the outward actions and adventure representing the inward struggle of the protagonists to grow and mature and become whole. In *The Farthest Shore* the inward struggle occurs in young prince Arren, Ged's companion. As Slusser says, "The physical journey may be read as a projection of Arren's fears, doubts and hopes" (43). The story is Arren's rather than Ged's, for Arren is destined to rule over all of Earthsea, and to be an effective ruler he must be whole.

As in his discussion of the previous two books, Slusser concentrates on imagery in this final volume. Besides spiders and shadows, he sees much dream imagery. Le Guin was intensely interested in dream research at this time of her life; *The Lathe of Heaven*, in which the entire plot revolves around dreams, was published the year before *The Farthest Shore*. But Slusser reserves his highest praise for the images in the last few chapters of the novel when Ged and Arren must cross the Land of the Dead. However, having thus reserved his praise, he gives few examples of the images that earn his admiration. He mentions the flight of the dragons, the self-sacrificial death of one great dragon, and Cob's desolation, but the concrete images of the Land of the Dead are glossed over with one reference to the Mountains of Pain. Rather than images, Slusser seems to be interested in themes. Once more life is found only in the acceptance of death. Because power shifts from the artist/wizard to a king at the end of the book, Slusser says Le Guin is confirming the primacy of the social realm. His final assessment of *The Farthest Shore* points out how different this fantasy is from most: "The thrust of this epic is not simply 'pre-Christian'; it is quite un-Christian, un-Western, in its naturalism, its reverence for the balance of life, and its refusal of transcendental values" (45).

Slusser's pamphlet is important as the first assessment of the trilogy as a whole. However, like many critics, in his determination to prove his thesis (that Taoism is the unifying factor in Le Guin's work), he discusses only those elements of the trilogy that fit into his thesis. In particular, his insistence on an allegorical interpretation of the novels directly contradicts the author's assertion that she dislikes allegory and certainly does not intend to write it:

> I hate allegories. A is "really" B and a hawk is "really" a handsaw — bah.
> Humbug. Any creation, primary or secondary, with any vitality to it, can
> "really" be a dozen mutually exclusive things at once, before breakfast.
> (*Language* 53)

This quote is peppered with allusions to Shakespeare, Dickens, Tolkien, and Lewis Carroll. Le Guin never talks down to her audience but rather assumes they are as well read as she is.

Another limitation of Slusser's analysis is that his interest in the trilogy is secondary to his interest in Le Guin's science fiction. He tends to discuss the Earthsea books in relation to the presumably more important science fiction rather than as valuable in and of themselves. On the other hand, he is one of the first science fiction critics to grant any value at all to the fantasy. He also fails to support some of his statements with evidence from the novels, thus weakening the force of his arguments. Nevertheless, Slusser's work is useful in laying the groundwork for much future criticism. He is often cited in articles about the trilogy, either as a supporting critic or as a straw man to be knocked over.

Another insightful critic entered the lists in 1977 by way of the humanities journal *Mosaic*. In "The Magic Art and the Evolution of Words: Ursula Le Guin's Earthsea Trilogy," T. A. Shippey argues that the trilogy is concerned with the changing historical perception of science, magic, and religion. Le Guin's anthropological background teaches her that these three words were once almost indistinguishable. However, modern use has given them hard and narrow meanings that create both problems and opportunities for a fantasy writer: the problems involve modern resistance to fantasy and the need to explain the fantasy elements, but the opportunities are to find ways to use fantasy to comment on modern reality, thus making fantasy relevant rather than escapist. Shippey feels that Le Guin takes full advantage of the opportunities in all three Earthsea books.

He explains that in *A Wizard of Earthsea* Le Guin establishes moral, intellectual, and physical limits for the magic of Earthsea, and she confines her characters within these limitations. As a wizard, Ged is very like a scientist, and he works within an anthropological framework. However, he is also the creative artist: only people with special talent can become wizards. The magic operates by what Shippey calls the "Rumpelstiltskin" theory; in other words, knowing the true name of a person or thing gives a wizard power over that person or thing. Shippey is fond of attaching familiar literary names to his ideas: he refers to Ged's first attempt to call up the spirit of a dead person as the "Sorcerer's Apprentice" scene and his second attempt as the "Dr. Faustus" scene. Shippey interprets *A Wizard of Earthsea* as Le Guin's rejection of Sir James Frazer's *The Golden Bough*, particularly as a correction of Frazer's view that early believers in magic and true names were savages who did not know the difference between a word and the thing it named. Whereas Frazer believed that things were superior to words, Le Guin gives equal respect to both, as well as great respect to the societies she creates, whose members are far from the distrustful savages about whom Frazer wrote. Ged's union with his shadow at the far reaches of the world is a rejection of Frazer's myth of the Fisher King, the king who must die to restore fertility to his wasted land.

While Shippey sees the first book of the trilogy as a discussion of science and magic, he views the second as a debate on the nature of religion. It is also a move from the unfamiliar to the familiar in that the Kargish people of Atuan are more like Americans than the inhabitants of the islands Ged considers home. The Kargs do not believe in magic, they have an organized religion and an organized state, and they live under a class system. Shippey also says the Kargs are more "like us" because they are white, which is surely an indirect statement about his own assumptions. As priestess, Tenar sees differing attitudes toward religion: some believe in the gods implicitly, some serve the gods for personal ends or pretend to believe in them for political reasons, and some are total atheists. Tenar herself has to struggle with belief. Whereas Frazer's attitude toward primitive religions is amused tolerance, Le Guin treats them with respect and even has Ged assure Tenar that her unnamed gods are real powers, though not real gods. For Le Guin, darkness and light have equal validity. Shippey concludes, however, that Le Guin agrees with Frazer that religion consists of a belief in supernatural powers and a desire to propitiate them.

According to Shippey, each book of the trilogy moves further into gloom and closer to familiar reality. When the magic begins to fail in *The Farthest Shore*, "Earthsea begins to resemble America in the aftermath of Vietnam: exhausted, distrustful, uncertain" (159). People turn to drugs and hypnosis for consolation. The view of eternal life presented in this novel seems almost blasphemous to a Christian reader, particularly in its presentation of Cob as a dark Christ, but Shippey defends Le Guin against willful blasphemy by showing parallels between the failure of magic in Earthsea and the failure of religion in modern America. (Apparently he presumes it cannot be blasphemous if it is metaphorical.) Like Slusser, Shippey makes much of the spider images in the book: "All suggest the entrapment of life in something powerful yet tenuous" (160). Shippey finds it significant that Ged, the restorer of true names, does not restore Cob's true name, but he never explains fully why he thinks this is significant.

Shippey concludes that the trilogy is a parable about modern life and that the parables are summed up in the gnomic statements of the mages, such as "To light a candle is to cast a shadow." But rather than acclaiming Le Guin as a mythopoeic writer, he finds her exactly the opposite:

> The truth, though, seems to be that she is at least as much of an iconoclast, a myth-breaker not a myth-maker. She rejects resurrection and eternal life; she refutes "cathartic" and "intellectualist" versions of an-

thropology alike; her relationship with Sir James Frazer in particular is one of correction too grave for parody . . . (163)

Unlike previous commentators on Le Guin, Shippey never mentions Taoism or Jungian psychology. His main interest is in early modern anthropology and the ways in which the trilogy addresses the ideas of the early anthropologists, particularly those of Frazer. Writing in St. John's College, Oxford, he exhibits the English attitude toward fantasy as a legitimate form of literature that requires no defense. His article is replete with casual references to C. S. Lewis, Christopher Marlowe, John Bunyan, and Dostoevsky, among other literary greats, with a casual assumption that Le Guin belongs in that company. He discusses her work as serious literature, not as what critics often see as the marginalized genre of children's fantasy. He also treats Le Guin as a respected anthropologist who has every right to correct or comment upon the views of earlier anthropologists. Shippey is clearly not one of the critics Le Guin accuses of "adult chauvinist piggery" (*Language* 54). Such an attitude is rare, as the next few years would show.

1979 was a banner year for Le Guin criticism. Not only did Putnam's publish her collection of essays, *The Language of the Night*, but two volumes of collected essays about her work also appeared. One, edited by Joe De Bolt, is entitled *Ursula K. Le Guin: Voyager to Inner Lands and to Outer Space*; the other, edited by Joseph D. Olander and Martin Harry Greenberg, was called simply *Ursula K. Le Guin*. Both are volumes in critical series, the De Bolt book in Kennikat Press's Literary Criticism Series and Olander and Greenberg in Taplinger's Writers of the 21st Century. The Kennikat collection contains eight essays, three of which deal with Earthsea. Of the nine essays in the other collection, only two discuss the fantasy trilogy. In both volumes the editors and contributors show more interest in Le Guin's science fiction than in her fantasy, but they make an obvious effort to give a modicum of attention to the Earthsea books, which had been grossly overlooked (to the embarrassment of guest editor Darko Suvin) in a special Le Guin issue of *Science-Fiction Studies* published in 1975. Science fiction critics were well aware that the trilogy was an important contribution to fantasy and to children's or young adult literature, but their own interests lay elsewhere; in these two collections of essays, they address the trilogy almost through a sense of duty. The reluctance shows in the quality of the essays. However, the simple fact that they do include Earthsea is evidence that the science fiction community felt a territorial claim on all of Le Guin's works. Certainly the children's literature critics who examined the trilogy never felt it their duty to drag Le Guin's science fiction into their discussion of her work. From the start of Le Guin's career the science fiction journals and magazines tried to review most of her work, except for the picture books and poetry.

The three essays on Earthsea in the De Bolt volume do not contribute great insights into the series; in fact, two of them show the effects of misapplied energies. Rollin A. Lasseter's article, ingenuously called "Four Letters about Le Guin," attempts to read the trilogy as a Christian work, an act in flagrant violation of the author's lifelong insistence that the closest thing she has to a religion is philosophical Taoism. Comparing Le Guin to Robert Louis Stevenson, Lasseter says that Le Guin's questioning of the dual nature of humanity in the Earthsea books provides a different answer than Stevenson's examination of dualism in *Dr. Jekyll and Mr. Hyde*. Stevenson splits his hero into two halves, one good and one evil, while Le Guin allows Ged to become whole through his acceptance of suffering and defeat and the knowledge of evil. Lasseter interprets Ged's shadow as evil, both individual and collective evil. In *A Wizard of Earthsea* the masculine spirit (represented by Ged) has to come to an understanding of its own capacity for evil. *The Tombs of Atuan* is about the journey of the feminine spirit (embodied by Tenar), which Lasseter equates with our capacity for joy. The only thing that can free the feminine spirit from the shadow is romantic love. *The Farthest Shore* is about the collective human shadow — the loss of hope. In his discussion of the third book, Lasseter becomes more and more allegorical, saying the land of the dead is really a representation of a hopeless reality, and restoring the king means "educating and empowering the governing will" (108). According to Lasseter, prince Arren experiences the dark night of the soul, a phrase associated with Christian mystics. In fairness to Lasseter, *The Farthest Shore* does lend itself to allegorical interpretation, especially when the inhospitable border between the living lands and the land of the dead is called the Mountains of Pain. But Le Guin insists there is no allegory in her work, particularly no Christian allegory. One insight Lasseter does contribute is to point out how rarely Le Guin addresses the journey of the feminine spirit in her works. Writing about the feminine was an internal conflict with which Le Guin was still struggling in the 1970s.

John R. Pfeiffer's essay in the 1979 De Bolt volume, "But Dragons Have Keen Ears: On Hearing Earthsea with Recollections of Beowulf," is the first article to approach the trilogy linguistically. Pfeiffer is interested in how Le Guin mimics the oral tradition of ancient epics like *Beowulf*. He views the themes, the cosmology, the climate, and the language of the trilogy as basically Germanic. Like *Beowulf*, *A Wizard of Earthsea* employs repetition, alliteration, a repertoire of linguistic formulas, kennings, gnomic utterances, lists, and a large percentage of dialogue. These are all qualities of an oral epic. Both works use the word "bright" many times over, share the same sense of fate, take place in island countries, and feature a major battle with dragons. However, some of Pfeiffer's evidence is sparse or faulty: while he is able to find many instances of alliteration in *A Wizard of Earthsea*, he can only find one kenning. Furthermore, he seems unaware of Le Guin's alternate identity as a poet; like Rudyard Kipling and other poet/fiction writers, Le Guin brings her poetic sense of language to her fiction. Her use of alliteration is not peculiar to *A Wizard of Earthsea*. The gnomic utterances Pfeiffer sees as Germanic are adapted from a book of Taoist philosophy. Despite his unfamiliarity with Le Guin's Taoist and Jungian philosophy, Pfeiffer's thoroughness is persuasive. Not only does he list seventeen specific instances of alliteration in *A Wizard of Earthsea*, but he also figures the percentage of dialogue in every chapter and compares it to the percentage of dialogue in *Beowulf*, the *Iliad*, the *Odyssey*, and the *Aeneid* — four epics composed for oral delivery. Although Le Guin's percentages are lower than those of the older epics, one of her chapters rings in at 47.4 percent dialogue, which approximates the percentage in the classical epics.

Pfeiffer reserves his final comments for the dragons. Because Le Guin says the stars speak the Old Speech — the language of Making — Pfeiffer concludes that the dragons must be identified with the stars. The dragons have created the world by means of the language of making. Ged not only learns to speak the Old Speech like the dragons, but he also learns to listen like a dragon, with keen ears that can hear from a great distance. This last section of the article seems to be the germ of a completely different essay; it does not fit well with the previous parts, which are unified by the comparison to *Beowulf*. Pfeiffer has read the Shippey article from *Mosaic*, but he seems unaware of other commentary on Earthsea. As inaccurate as some of his conclusions are, he is the first person to stress the orality of the trilogy and to point out its resemblance to *Beowulf*.

The final essay on Earthsea in *Ursula K. Le Guin: Voyager to Inner Lands and to Outer Space* considers the trilogy as children's literature. Francis J. Molson's "The Earthsea Trilogy: Ethical Fantasy for Children" attempts to coin a new term for a certain type of fantasy that others call heroic fantasy or high fantasy. Molson wants to call it ethical fantasy, partly because it is not always heroic in the traditional sense and partly because the new term does not invite invidious comparisons between "low" and "high" fantasy. Moreover, these fantasies incorporate their authors' complex philosophies and values in an attempt to teach ethics through entertainment:

> Ethical fantasy, as it has emerged in contemporary children's literature, dramatizes several interrelated propositions whose continuing validity is taken for granted: making ethical choices, whether deliberate or not, is

central in the lives of young people; actions do bear consequences not only for oneself but for society, and sometimes apparently insignificant actions can bring about momentous consequences; maturity involves accepting responsibility for one's actions; and character bespeaks destiny.

(130)

According to Molson, ethical fantasy is didactic without being moralizing. The ethics go down with a spoonful of sugar. Fantasy writers blend the old and the new in an entertaining manner. They pull elements from traditional literature which will be familiar to their readers, then add their own vision and creativity to come up with something different. Molson sees ethical fantasy as a recent development in children's literature, resulting from the sudden absence of shared religious beliefs. Religion used to teach ethics to children, but in contemporary times fantasy seeks to fill the gap. Modern fantasy also incorporates an understanding of psychology that was unavailable to earlier writers of children's literature.

Molson points out that Ged's heroics are quite different from those of traditional heroes. When he takes responsibility for his shadow or persuades Tenar to leave her labyrinth, he is showing the child reader that maturity includes taking responsibility for one's own actions and for others' well-being. Without making reference to *Dr. Jekyll and Mr. Hyde*, Molson divides Ged into two beings, calling the shadow "Sparrowhawk" (the name by which Ged is generally known) and the main character "Ged" (his true name, known to only a few trusted friends). The Sparrowhawk part of him is fiercely independent and arrogant, whereas the Ged part recognizes the need for others and the need to help others. The same ethical theme permeates *The Tombs of Atuan*, where Tenar has to learn a similar lesson. Tenar's ethical dilemma is whether to follow her training and kill Ged for violating her sacred labyrinth or to deny everything she knows and trust this stranger. Just as Ged is divided in two by his true name and his use name, so is Tenar. She has one name she is known by, Arha (the Eaten One), and the true name she has forgotten until Ged restores it to her. For Molson, Arha represents the dark side of the priestess, while Tenar is her true whole being. Molson sees Ged's attitude toward Tenar as brotherly, precluding any possible romantic attachment. Thus Ged takes Tenar to his old master Ogion because he feels she needs a parent and Ogion is the closest thing to a father in his own life.

Whereas Molson sees Ged's coming-of-age and Tenar's as a kind of rebirth, prince Arren's coming-of-age in *The Farthest Shore* is more traditional in that he is simply claiming his destiny to be king. In fact, the true quest of the third book is to restore the kingship, not to repair the hole Cob has made in the world. Ged's true quest is individuation; he is in his middle years in *The Farthest Shore*, which is the natural time for Jungian individuation. This is the reason for Ged's self-doubts in the last book: he is questioning his past choices and seeking to take the next step toward selfhood. The nature of these quests cannot help but burden the book with weightier dialogue than the previous two books. Some critics have seen this as a weakness. If so, says Molson, it is a necessary one.

Unlike other critics in science fiction volumes, Molson is knowledgeable about children's literature and about previous criticism of the Earthsea trilogy. Endnotes include citations to Eleanor Cameron's article, Le Guin's essays, and a British article on teaching *Wizard*. Molson's close reading of the trilogy is for the most part accurate and remains focused on ethical considerations. The only questionable point has to do with the dualities of character in Ged and Tenar. Molson's approach works well enough with Ged, who does incorporate his "Sparrowhawk" persona and become whole, but Tenar never embraces the "Arha" part of herself — to do so would be to deny life and freedom. Ged must unite with his dark self to become whole, while Tenar must repudiate her dark self. Molson fails to see the difference here. Also, he is unable to bring Arren into this model of dualism. While Arren wrestles with his fear of death and his unbelief, he never confronts a shadow side of equal strength. However, the trilogy certainly fits Molson's description of ethical fantasy. Unfortunately, this term has not caught on. Most of the fantasies Molson categorizes as ethical are still referred to as high fantasy. Perhaps if this article had been published in a children's literature journal it would have had greater impact. Few critics of children's literature pick up volumes of science fiction essays. Perhaps, too, ethical fantasy seems too narrow a term to critics since it would exclude fantasy that contains no didactic moral element. The only writers Molson lists in this subgenre are C. S. Lewis, Lloyd Alexander, Madeleine L'Engle, Susan Cooper, and J. R. R. Tolkien — an elite list.

The two articles in the other 1979 volume, Olander and Greenberg's *Ursula K. Le Guin*, are of more consistent quality and present a more unified critical approach. Margaret P. Esmonde's "The Master Pattern: The Psychological Journey in the Earthsea Trilogy" takes as its thesis that the basic pattern of the trilogy is Jungian. Esmonde is aware of Slusser's comments on the trilogy, but she states that there is a dearth of other criticism on Earthsea because it is both fantasy and children's literature, neither of which is taken seriously by literary critics. Since children's literature criticism was still in its infancy in 1979, Esmonde can be forgiven for being unaware of it. She has clearly read other Le Guin works, particularly the essays "The Child and the Shadow" and an early version of "Why Are Americans Afraid of Dragons?"

Esmonde's interpretation sees all three books as stages in an individual's progress toward individuation, which in its final phase involves total integration of personality. In *A Wizard of Earthsea*, Ged represents the Jungian ego and his mentor Ogion represents the archetype Jung called the Wise Old Man. Ogion fulfills this archetype completely, leading Ged through the self-questioning necessary for the adolescent ego and assisting him in his quest for individuation. Ogion even carries out the Wise Old Man's optional task of providing something tangible to help the seeker on his journey; in this case, Ogion fashions a new wizard's staff for Ged. When Ged gives his shadow his own name and accepts that dark part of himself, he achieves his Jungian goal of maturity.

The Tombs of Atuan deals with a feminine form of individuation. Esmonde points out that the plot of this second volume parallels the story of Theseus in the Minotaur's labyrinth. Tenar plays the role of Ariadne, who helps Theseus escape. Taking a mythological approach to the Theseus legend, Esmonde suggests it is actually a version of the mythic seasonal cycle, in which the Sun king escapes his ritual winter death with the assistance of the goddess Aphrodite. So, to Esmonde, Tenar is both Ariadne and Aphrodite. Like Ariadne, Tenar uses a ball of thread to navigate her labyrinth, and like Aphrodite, she is associated with apples, which also have a biblical connection as well as a connection to the fairy tale "Snow White." Esmonde mines every possible aspect of these connections, showing how Ged is associated with light (like the Sun king) and how the evil priestess Kossil operates as a wicked stepmother. Curiosity and sexual desire lead Tenar to help Ged and abandon the only life she has known. Like Ged, Tenar finally accepts the dark part of herself and becomes whole. The process is more passive than Ged's experience because Tenar is almost pure Shadow and faces the problem of integrating the more active ego.

According to Esmonde, in *The Farthest Shore* Arren is the one traveling toward psychological wholeness. Since it deals with death, this volume is necessarily more philosophical than the first two. In order to make such an incomprehensible subject understandable, Le Guin structures this book as more of a traditional hero adventure, thus adding a note of familiarity for readers used to stories about heroic young princes who must prove their right to the throne. Like those traditional princes, Arren has a wise magician to counsel him and a magic sword at his side. However, unlike those heroes, Arren succeeds not by conquering hordes of evil warriors, but by conquering his own fear of death. To Esmonde, as to other critics, Le Guin's land of death looks like a classical Hades, and rather than a physical journey through this dry land, Esmonde interprets Ged and Arren's trek through the land of the dead as a projection of their spirits. Just as in the first two books, the protagonist finds wholeness and returns to the land of the living ready for kingship.

The most important point that Esmonde makes is that in all three books the crucial turning point rests on an act of trust. In *A Wizard of Earthsea*, when Ged is at his lowest point of self-loathing, his friend Vetch freely gives him the gift of Vetch's true name. This is a supreme act of trust, for the name magic that operates in Earthsea gives one complete power over another person through his or her true name. Similarly, Ged not only gives Tenar her own true name, but he also trusts her with his own at a time when he has no guarantee that she will help him. Ged's trust enables Tenar to learn to trust. In the final book, the mutual trust between Ged and Arren is thoroughly tested, but Arren's choice to trust Ged leads to the healing of all Earthsea.

Esmonde ties the Jungian theme to Le Guin's science fiction books as well. All of Le Guin's protagonists must take this "psychological journey through pain and fear to integration" (34). This archetypal journey is the basic pattern of all of Le Guin's fiction. As far as the Earthsea trilogy is concerned, Esmonde's interpretation works best with the first book. In order to fit the second and third volumes into the same Jungian frame-work, she has to manipulate the evidence slightly. Ged faces a clear Shadow in *A Wizard of Earthsea*, but the other two main characters do not have such a clear-cut opposition to integrate. By limiting herself to the Shadow archetype as the basic pattern of the novels, Esmonde necessarily limits her psychological interpretation of the story.

Margaret Esmonde is one of several critics who have gone on to build scholarly reputations at least partly on articles about Le Guin. Esmonde later published several other articles on Le Guin, discussing the concept of death in *The Farthest Shore* in publications such as *Fantasiae* (a science fiction and fantasy newsletter) and *Horn Book*, the premier journal of children's literature. Esmonde also reviewed critical works about Le Guin. Two of her later articles deal with *The Farthest Shore* as an exemplum of modern children's fantasy about death and the hereafter. Other children's literature critics also took up the theme of death in children's fantasy and discussed Le Guin's trilogy, in particular *The Farthest Shore*, among other works of fantasy. These articles often discussed how death, a staple in nineteenth-century children's literature, had become a taboo subject in twentieth-century books for young readers until the 1970s. By that decade writers felt free to explore non-Christian views of death and the afterlife. Le Guin in particular is viewed as a writer with a grim but honest personal vision of the afterlife. However, these are articles about death in children's fiction, not articles about Le Guin. Many other general articles and reviews that discuss children's fantasy also mention the Earthsea trilogy as a major work in the field. Unlike Esmonde, none of these later critics have felt it incumbent upon them to tie Le Guin's adult science fiction to her fantasy for young readers, but in 1979 Esmonde was writing mainly for the science fiction audience.

The second essay in Olander and Greenberg's collection solves the problem of fitting the trilogy into a Jungian framework in a different way. In "Words of Binding: Patterns of Integration in the Earthsea Trilogy," John H. Crow and Richard D. Erlich take a Jungian approach similar to Esmonde's, but they interpret Tenar as Ged's Anima — the feminine side of him. In their view, Ged's process of individuation incorporates the first step of accepting the Shadow, the second step of descending into the underworld to rescue the Anima, and the final step of maturing into the Wise Old Man. In the first book Ged represents the archetype of the Child while Ogion is the Wise Old Man; by making Ged the Wise Old Man in the final book, Le Guin completes a circular pattern. This interpretation sees all three books as steps in Ged's individuation: "Ged's return to Gont on the back of the ancient dragon suggests an alliance with the spirit and a completion of the Self in the final process of individuation" (203).

Crow and Erlich posit two other structural patterns in the trilogy besides a Jungian one: a movement from social disorder to order, and the balance of opposites. The main balance is between life and death; the former involves change and the passage of time, whereas the latter is timeless and changeless. Each protagonist must learn to balance internal forces (obligations to oneself) with external forces (obligations to society). Crow and Erlich also see a balance between Le Guin's Jungian views and a certain Sartrean existentialism. Earthsea operates in an existential arena where there are no certainties other than death and no heaven to reward the just. The inhabitants of Earthsea are as prone to despair and hopelessness as are modern Americans.

According to these two critics, Tenar gives up her personal identity in order to serve her society, but the religious cult over which she presides is outdated even in her culture, where religious evolution has branched off from worship of Tenar's Nameless Ones toward a more self-serving belief in a masculine Godking. The labyrinth of Atuan represents the forces of the unconscious, often associated with the feminine. Tenar serves a long-vanished past, and Ged must teach her to live in the present. Prince Arren, on the other hand, has to learn the opposite lesson — not to look toward the future and the hope of immortality. As Crow and Erlich put it, "The contrast between Arha [Tenar's name as priestess] and Arren, then, is the contrast of being controlled by the weight of the past, embodied in public tradition, and being controlled by the fear of the future, motivated by private concern . . . " (207). Only Ged makes choices based on a thoughtful balance of past and future. The choices he has made in the past have both created the person he has become and limited his choices for the future.

Crow and Erlich see Le Guin's dragons as symbolic of Jung's concept of the spirit. They are associated with the elements of spirit, wind, and fire. Like the Jungian spirit, dragons cannot be fully comprehended but only partially understood as manifested through their actions. Both exist outside human judgment and knowledge. Moreover, dragons represent a state of being, whereas humans live in a state of doing. The problem of being and doing is central to Le Guin's work. The land of the dead is associated with being while the living lands are associated with doing. Human existence, or being, precedes action, but action is necessary in order to create being. Crow and Erlich see this as a paradox in Le Guin. Each act binds a person to previous acts and limits future acts. This requires the practice of a kind of heroic restraint known in Taoism as *wu-wei*, loosely meaning taking only necessary action.

To Crow and Erlich, Cob is not so much an evil wizard as a mad scientist with the power to destroy the world. He represents a collective fear of death. Ged, on the other hand, is the developing Self. As these critics put it, "Ged's return to the isle of Gont completes the pattern in the trilogy, which presents the hero as an archetypal representative of man's psychological journey from the birth of consciousness to the complete integration of the Self at the end of the process of individuation" (215). The development of the individual, in this case Ged, always precedes and takes precedence over the development of society. Le Guin always balances the needs of the individual to the needs of her or his society, but she clearly favors the former. She also favors the balance of ends and means; unless the two are unified, no action should be taken.

Crow and Erlich's essay is a thoughtful and comprehensive analysis of the trilogy. Their Jungian interpretation works better than Esmonde's, and they make telling points about Le Guin's tendency toward existentialism. The essay loses its focus only in the final pages, where the authors turn to Le Guin's science fiction in an attempt to prove that all of her works share the same outlook and structure. This part of the essay degenerates into an apologia for the trilogy, as if it must be measured by a supposedly more superior science fiction. This defensive attitude toward the trilogy is shared by most articles published in science fiction journals and collections. Having staked out Le Guin's work as their territory, the science fiction critics often try to rope in her fantasy and realistic fiction as well, but the resistance many hard-core science fiction readers feel toward other genres tends to keep the apologists on the defensive. There is no such defensive tone in the children's literature criticism other than the early defensive posture toward fantasy as escapism, a charge that had generally faded by the 1980s.

Another ground-breaking article appeared in Ball State University's journal *Forum* in 1979. In "Bright the Hawk's Flight: The Journey of the Hero in Ursula Le Guin's Earthsea Trilogy," Virginia L. White, who had published previously in the field of children's literature, introduces the ideas of Joseph Campbell into Le Guin criticism. Campbellian interpretations were an inevitable development for the trilogy; Campbell's *The Hero with a Thousand Faces* works so well with fantasy that every major fantasist eventually receives the treatment. White interprets the trilogy in terms of Campbell's monomyth about the classic journey of the mythic hero, which is broken down into three stages: departure, initiation, and return. The hero hears a call to adventure, accepts or rejects it, faces trials and tasks either alone or with supernatural help (including a descent into the underworld), and eventually returns home with a reward that will be of service to his community. According to White, this pattern incorporates the entire trilogy, with *A Wizard of Earthsea* representing the hero's departure, *The Tombs of Atuan* as the initiation stage, and *The Farthest Shore* as the hero's return. Beneath this overarching structure, each book recreates the entire pattern in miniature, so that in book one Ged goes through all three stages, in the second book Tenar accomplishes the journey, and in the third, Arren succeeds as the hero.

All three protagonists at first resist the call to adventure, but each eventually succumbs. In *A Wizard of Earthsea* Ged experiences three calls to adventure: the first as a child when he uses a spell to call goats to him, the second when he defends his village from invaders by calling up a fog, and the third as a student at Roke when he calls up the spirit of a dead woman. In all three cases, Ged resists the call to adventure. White's interpretation is problematic in that her choices of calls to adventure are inconsistent; one could easily choose three other incidents in Ged's youth as his calls to adventure. Ged brings the call to adventure to the other two protagonists in the series, and in both cases they too refuse the call. Indeed, Arren is at first quick to accept the call, but he later falters and comes close to refusing. Tenar, on the other hand, is like Ged in resisting the initial call but later succumbing to its lure.

Within this structure, White emphasizes a recurring theme of the reconciliation of opposites — a theme other critics have discussed before her. She also points out many specific usages of light and dark imagery in the trilogy; again, others have preceded her. However, she is the first to point out that in the final volume the dark and light images are replaced by mixed images of dusk, representing the loss of balance in Earthsea under Cob's curse. The main importance of White's article is that it introduces

Campbell's monomyth into Le Guin criticism. Later critics, especially in the field of children's literature, would pick up this theme and develop it further. Campbell's ideas are useful in any discussion of fantasy; indeed, many teachers use them as a framework in teaching fantasy.

No year that followed ever surpassed 1979 for sheer number of articles about Le Guin, but from then on there was a steady trickle of criticism that continues to this day. In 1980 David Rees included an essay on Le Guin in his book *The Marble in the Water: Essays on Contemporary Writers of Fiction for Children and Young Adults*. Rees, a British critic of children's literature, seldom praises the subjects of his essays; he tends to be hypercritical about fantasy writers who write for young readers. But in the case of Le Guin, he finds little to carp about. In "Earthsea Revisited" he directs his scorn at all the mythic interpretations of the trilogy rather than at the author herself. He is concerned with tying the trilogy to the real world, finding the books rich in associations that will be meaningful to young readers. Indeed, he compares Le Guin's wealth of associations to the work of T. S. Eliot rather than to other children's writers.

Rees sees the invasion of Ged's homeland as reminiscent of Viking attacks on Saxon England, the process of choosing a new high priestess as similar to the search for a new Dalai Lama, the selection of the Archmage as a reflection of the college of cardinals choosing a pope, the story of the labyrinth as a retelling of the legend of the Minotaur, and the school for wizards on Roke Island as Oxford or Cambridge. Sometimes Rees's connections are extreme, as when he discusses associations with the characters' names: "Arren/Aaron, high priest; Ged/good (even God?); and Tenar is one letter short of an anagram of 'renata,' Italian for reborn, as well as suggesting tenacity or the French 'tenir,' to hold" (79). Rees either ignores or is unaware of Le Guin's repudiation of the association of Ged and god as early as her 1973 article "Dreams Must Explain Themselves."

Rees also sees the trilogy implicitly as young adult literature concerned with the problems of adolescence. All the books deal with growing up in some fashion; the first and third volumes deal expressly with a traditionally masculine kind of growing up, and the second volume with a feminine kind. The masculine world is a world of action and travel while the feminine world is passive and land-locked. This aspect of Le Guin's approach is conservative, unlike contemporary children's books that blur gender distinctions. Le Guin's elitism (seen in her choice of uniquely talented individuals as protagonists) is similarly conservative in an age that stresses a democratic approach to building children's self-esteem. In *A Wizard of Earthsea*, growing up means recognizing and accepting the capacity for evil within oneself. For Tenar growing up means coming to terms with her femininity and sexuality, whereas for Arren it is learning to listen to wiser adults. In fact, the whole trilogy differs from modern children's literature by its inclusion of wise and stable adult figures.

Rees's final point is that the Earthsea trilogy is more concerned with nature than with myth. It abounds with specific descriptions of nature, the Equilibrium is basically a conservationist's ecological view of nature, and humankind's ability to disrupt the balance of nature reflects contemporary American society. Magic, says Rees, really plays a very small part in the books. Rees seems to be intent on proving that the Earthsea books are more closely linked to contemporary realism than to fantasy. This may be an attempt to raise the literary reputation of the books, since modern literature prizes realistic fiction more highly than fantasy. The comparison to T. S. Eliot may have the same purpose. Although as a British critic Rees probably takes fantasy quite seriously, this volume of essays was published in Boston for an American readership that still tended to dismiss fantasy as escapism.

Jeanne Murray Walker, another critic who has built a reputation partly on commentary about Le Guin, published her first significant Le Guin criticism in *Mosaic* in 1980. Her article, "Rites of Passage Today: The Cultural Significance of *A Wizard of Earthsea*," proposes that high fantasy allows teen readers to experience a coming-of-age ritual by proxy. Modern American society fails to provide this mark of adulthood for its young people, yet the rite of passage is a vital part of every society. The ritual marks a young person's change of status in symbolic form, usually involving a symbolic death and rebirth. Ged's rite of passage at the end of the first chapter in *A Wizard of Earthsea* summarizes and foreshadows the action of the rest of the book:

> The spring through which Ged wades is an analogue for the ocean on which he later completes his troubled quest for the shadow. The shadows which "slid and mingled" at the initiation anticipate the terrible shadow which later enters the world by Ged's hand. The new name that Ogion whispers to the boy precedes his ultimate naming of the shadow by that name. The central role of Ogion at the initiation predicts his crucial role in healing the wounded sparrowhawk, the form magically assumed by Ged in his flight from deadly peril. Ged's isolation during his walk through the spring prefigures his years of physical and psychological loneliness. (183)

Such a short ritual in itself could not take a reader through a proxy experience, but the fact that the ritual is played out through the plot of the novel allows the significance to sink in for the reader. The novel is about the individual finding a place within the social order.

Walker makes much of metaphors. Magic is a metaphor for the interrelationship between nature and society; naming is a metaphor for the interrelationship of nature and society with the individual. Like all high fantasy, the book dramatizes the rite of passage, but unlike other fantasies, in this book the actual ritual appears. Since fantasy descends from medieval romance, a romance structure underlies the genre, showing the hero acting against the background of a social structure. According to Walker, high fantasy thus plays a vital role in the individual's life and in society's life, bridging a gap between childhood and adulthood. In later articles, Walker extends the argument about the value of a vicarious rite of passage for American youth. Without a shared set of religious values, the only shared value in American society is materialism, and fantasy shows alternative sets of values.

Walker's intelligent analysis of rites of passage contributes more to Le Guin criticism than do the many pedagogical articles that stress developmental needs; however, her arguments only apply to a small segment of the adolescent population — those who read fantasy. The majority of young adults must find their vicarious rites of passage elsewhere. In many ways, Walker's comments are simply another apologia for fantasy. The same could be said for the special Le Guin issue of *Extrapolation*, which also appeared in 1980. As if intent on making up for the omission of Earthsea criticism in the Le Guin issue of *Science-Fiction Studies*, this other major science fiction journal devoted its Fall issue to incorporating the fantasy novels into Le Guin's science fiction oeuvre. Again, the overarching attitude is slightly defensive and occasionally patronizing.

Three of the articles in this special issue deserve mention. Edgar C. Bailey, Jr.'s "Shadows in Earthsea: Le Guin's Use of a Jungian Archetype" is in many ways derivative of other discussions of Jung's influence on Le Guin. However, Bailey makes two telling points. In *Wizard*, Ged's problems with Jasper, a fellow student, stem from Ged's projecting his Jungian Shadow onto Jasper, seeing in the other boy all the arrogance and pride Ged cannot recognize in himself. Ged is the real instigator of the hostility that develops between the two. Later, when Ged follows a sailor who has offered to guide him to shelter, the shadow, which has possessed the sailor, is effectively acting as a spiritual guide. Part of the role of the Shadow archetype is to guide one into the deepest, darkest part of the psyche.

Extrapolation's Le Guin issue also contains an article by Thomas J. Remington, "A Time to Live and a Time to Die: Cyclical Renewal in the Earthsea Trilogy." Remington's thesis is that all the important events in the trilogy are linked to seasonal celebrations in Earthsea. Although he stretches his thesis past the point of credibility in his discussion of *The Tombs of Atuan*, his close reading of the books contributes interesting insights. For example, in *A Wizard of Earthsea*, the shadow is loosed the day after the Long Dance, which is the night of the summer solstice. Ged's confrontation with the shadow takes place right after Sunreturn, the first day of the new year. Thus, Le Guin is using the Fisher King myth of seasonal regeneration. Remington sees the same pattern in *Tombs*, but he finds it inverted in *The Farthest Shore*.

The most influential article in this issue of the journal is C. N. Manlove's "Conservatism in the Fantasy of Le Guin." Pointing out that fantasy is basically a conservative genre that "looks to the past to sustain the nature and values of the present," Manlove describes conservatism in the trilogy as a concern with balance, moderation, and celebration of the status quo. Balance shows itself mainly through the Equilibrium, the deep-seated balance of the world, which wizards are sworn to protect. Even the structure of *Wizard* is balanced: three chapters tell of the shadow's pursuit of Ged, then three chapters show Ged's pursuit of the shadow. The use of the number nine also contributes to the balance of the books. There are nine master wizards at the school for wizards and nine great runes, Ged and the shadow chase each other for nine months, the constellation representing the Rune of Ending is shaped like a nine and has nine stars, and Ged's journeys in the first volume trace out a figure nine on the map of Earthsea. In the third book, Ged's journey follows a reversed and upside-down nine. Thus, Manlove finds it appropriate that "[u]nder the aegis of the reversed nine in *The Farthest Shore*... Ged's magical power is steadily unwound until at the end he leaves Roke as a mere man" (290).

To Manlove, even the magic in the trilogy is conservative and moderate. There are limits to magic, and its primary use is to right imbalances in the Equilibrium, in effect restoring the status quo. Wizards want to keep things as they are. This differs from Le Guin's science fiction, in which change is valued. In the fantasy books Le Guin is expressing her own joy in unchanging creation.

Manlove is cited regularly by critics who came after him. His arguments are persuasive and well supported. Most of his insights are original, unlike those in the raft of articles that compare Le Guin to Tolkien or to C. S. Lewis. One comparative essay that does contain some originality is Doris T. Myers's "'True Speech' in the Fantasies of Tolkien and Le Guin," published in *Forum Linguisticum* in 1982. Myers is interested in what she calls our "language archetype": assumptions that older languages are more perfect than newer ones, that language helps control the universe, and that names are the most important aspect of language. This "myth of true speech" is used differently by Le Guin and Tolkien. Le Guin's use of the myth is influenced by American anthropological linguistics and Taoism, whereas Tolkien bases his on European philology.

The Old Speech in Earthsea fits perfectly into the myth of true speech. Tolkien invents many more languages, but instead of presenting one true name for every person and thing, as Le Guin does, Tolkien provides multiple names; therefore, language as a means of control and power is not as vital to Tolkien as to Le Guin. Both authors, however, stress the aesthetic qualities of names.

While critics were churning out dozens of journal articles in the early 1980s, graduate students were mining Le Guin's works for theses and dissertations — another indication of literary respectability — and series editors started commissioning volumes on Le Guin. Published monographs aimed at a general audience usually contributed nothing new to Le Guin criticism, and the writers of these volumes tended to be science fiction critics with little knowledge of children's or young adult literature. One of the best of the monographs is Charlotte Spivack's Twayne volume on Le Guin, published in 1984. (Like most of the single-author studies of Le Guin, it is titled simply *Ursula K. Le Guin.*) Although ignorant of children's literature, Spivack has a respectful attitude toward the trilogy and explores its themes and images as carefully as she examines the adult works. Spivack lists recurring images in the Earthsea books: birds, dragons, stones, light and dark imagery, and the central image of webs. Occasionally Spivack wanders onto Freudian territory, saying, for example, that Ged's entrance into Tenar's underground labyrinth is a symbolic rape, but she is more interested in structural motifs, seeing *Tombs* as a retelling of both the Theseus story and the tale of Persephone and identifying the wizards' Immanent Grove as the Norse Yggdrasil, or sacred tree at the center of the world. As an aside, she also points out that for a man who preaches the value of contemplation, Ged in *The Farthest Shore* is extremely active.

Although science fiction critics had finally discovered the trilogy in the wake of Robert Scholes, children's literature critics continued to pursue Earthsea independently. Lois Kuznets, a highly respected scholar of children's literature, published a comparative essay on Le Guin, Lloyd Alexander, and Susan Cooper in the noted journal *The Lion and the Unicorn* in 1985. "'High Fantasy' in America: A Study of Lloyd Alexander, Ursula Le Guin, and Susan Cooper" takes issue with Brian Attebery's history of fantasy, *The Fantasy Tradition in American Literature, from Irving to Le Guin* (1980), dismissing it as too vague and limited. Attebery claims that the Earthsea trilogy is "the most challenging and richest American fantasy to date" (162). He sees *A Wizard of Earthsea* as an amalgam of several story types, the sorcerer's apprentice and the Russian fairy tale as dissected by Propp, while *The Tombs of Atuan* is a rescue tale and *The Farthest Shore* is a quest. One interesting sidelight of his analysis is his contention that the geography of the island of Atuan is modeled after Oregon. Attebery commends Le Guin's work as the apogee of American fantasy.

Kuznets does not argue with Attebery's analysis of Le Guin, but rather with his historic account of the development of American fantasy. Her own approach to the three children's authors she wishes to compare is to explore their use of the Arthurian myth of male adolescent development, which "depicts an adolescent rite of passage in terms of the quest of an unacknowledged son for the phallic sword and/or uterine cauldron or grail" so that he may restore fertility to the land (27). As far as the trilogy is concerned, Kuznets sees Ged as a Merlin-figure and Arren as an Arthur-figure. Kuznets's most telling points are that *Tombs* is not particularly feminist, in that it becomes the story of a maiden in distress and depicts the suppression of a female cult, and that most readers fail to notice that the sympathetic characters in the Earthsea books are usually dark-skinned. Kuznets sees Le Guin's casual adoption of Native American or African American physical characteristics as an important statement.

In the following year another children's literature critic, Cordelia Sherman, contributed a few new insights on Le Guin in an article published in the *Children's Literature Association Quarterly*. Although her comparative analysis of the trilogy and George MacDonald's Curdie books does not hold together throughout the article, she rightly points out that they share a common purpose: "to teach children by dramatic example what it means to be a good adult" (24). Sherman stresses that the shadow is not evil in and of itself, though many critics perceive it to be. The evil stems from Ged's not restraining the shadow. Nor are the Nameless Ones in *Tombs* evil; they are powerful, ancient, and amoral. In comparing the vibrant life of the school for (male) wizards to the stagnant female cult of the Nameless Ones, Sherman says, "The subliminal message of *The Tombs of Atuan* seems to be that women living without men must become twisted and purposeless, while men living without women can be productive and strong" (26). However, as a character, Tenar is just as psychologically complex as Le Guin's male protagonists and takes an active role in her own rescue.

By the late 1980s, Le Guin criticism was awash with articles about Taoism, Jungian archetypes, mythic sources, and literary influences and comparisons. So many critics covered the same ground that astute scholars began to look for new territory to explore. One, M. Teresa Tavormina, noticed that classical influences had yet to be addressed in detail. In "A Gate of Horn and Ivory: Dreaming True and False in Earthsea," Tavormina focuses on how Le Guin transforms a specific passage in Virgil's *Aeneid* into a central image. The passage has to do with the back door to Hell, called the Gates of Sleep, which has two portals: the ivory gate is the means by which false dreams enter the world of the living, and the gate of horn provides egress for true dreams. On the island of Roke, the school for wizards has a magical portal which at first appears to be made of wood, but when Ged has finally surrendered his name to the doorkeeper in order to get in, he turns and sees that the doorway is made of ivory and the door itself of polished horn. Readers later learn that this is the back door to the school. Tavormina does not believe that Le Guin wishes to equate the school with Virgil's Hell, but she does see a connection to the twin gates that send forth true and false dreams. Unlike Virgil, however, Le Guin does not accept that dreams can be separated into true or false, so she combines Virgil's two gates into one. This is another instance of Le Guin's integration of opposites, which critics have found in all of her works. At the end of *Wizard*, when Ged has incorporated his shadow and is starting home, he sees the new moon as "a ring of ivory, a rim of horn" (*Wizard* 194). To Tavormina, this signifies Ged's reentry into life by way of the gates of dream.

Although Tavormina's essay is thought-provoking, her interpretation of Le Guin's use of the gates of horn and ivory does not fully satisfy the reader whose thought has been provoked. Why Le Guin has chosen this image and what she means to suggest by it are not thoroughly explicated. On the other hand, the fact that no previous scholar had noticed this image implies that there are yet unplumbed depths in the trilogy. Few were to plumb those depths with the assurance that they were discussing a finished series. Tavormina's article came out in 1988; in 1990, Le Guin threw a wrench into the works by publishing *Tehanu: The Last Book of Earthsea*, which necessarily altered critics' perception of the Earthsea books. Since Le Guin's own altered perceptions between 1972, when the "trilogy" was finished, and 1990, when it became a tetralogy, underwent a drastic change provoked by developments in the science fiction field, a discussion of the final book must be postponed for a later chapter.

One article that postdates *Tehanu* yet ignores its impact on the series is Craig and Diana Barrow's "Le Guin's Earthsea: Voyages in Conciousness [*sic*]," which appeared in *Extrapolation* in 1991. A mish-mash of Freudianism, anthropology, Campbellian monomyth, and Jungian archetypes, the article nevertheless makes important connections between the trilogy and the work of Le Guin's anthropologist father, Alfred Kroeber, among the Californian Indian tribes. Name magic, the importance of dreams, and Tenar's religious rituals are concepts Le Guin may have gleaned from her father's work. The Barrows also point out that Ged is an abandoned child who tries to substitute power for love. Their interpretation of Ged's actions is more complex than that of most commentators, who tend to attribute Ged's difficulties to simple arrogance. Although the Barrows concede the existence of *Tehanu*, they examine only the first three books of the series. None of the scholars who followed them would be able to ignore that troublesome final volume.

Works Cited

Alexander, Lloyd. *The Black Cauldron*. New York: Holt, 1965.

——. *The Book of Three*. New York: Holt, 1964.

——. *The Castle of Llyr*. New York: Holt, 1966.

Attebery, Brian. *The Fantasy Tradition in American Literature: From Irving to Le Guin*. Bloomington: Indiana UP, 1980.

Bailey, Edgar C., Jr. "Shadows in Earthsea: Le Guin's Use of a Jungian Archetype." *Extrapolation* 21 (Fall 1980): 254–61.

Barbour, Douglas. "On Ursula Le Guin's 'A Wizard of Earthsea.'" *Riverside Quarterly* 6 (April 1974): 119–23.

Barrow, Craig and Diana. "Le Guin's Earthsea: Voyages in Conciousness [*sic*]." *Extrapolation* 32 (Spring 1991): 20–44.

Campbell, Joseph. *The Hero with a Thousand Faces*. Princeton: Princeton UP, 1953.

Cameron, Eleanor. "High Fantasy: *A Wizard of Earthsea*." *Crosscurrents of Criticism: Horn Book Essays 1968–1977*. Ed. Paul Heins. Boston: Horn Book, 1977. 333–41.

Crow, John H., and Richard D. Erlich. "Words of Binding: Patterns of Integration in the Earthsea Trilogy." *Ursula K. Le Guin*. Ed. Joseph D. Olander and Martin Harry Greenberg. Writers of the 21st Century Series. New York: Taplinger, 1979. 200–24.

Esmonde, Margaret P. "Beyond the Circles of the World: Death and the Hereafter in Children's Literature." *Webs and Wardrobes: Humanist and Religious World Views in Children's Literature*. Ed. Joseph O'Beirne and Lucy Floyd Morcock Milner. Lanham, MD: UP of America, 1987. 34–45.

——. "The Gift of Men: Death and Deathlessness in Children's Fantasy." *Fantasiae* 7.9 (April 1979): 1, 8–11.

——. "The Master Pattern: The Psychological Journey in the Earthsea Trilogy." *Ursula K. Le Guin*. Ed. Joseph D. Olander and Martin Harry Greenberg. Writers of the 21st Century Series. New York: Taplinger, 1979. 15–35.

Fox, Geoff, ed. "Notes on 'Teaching' *A Wizard of Earthsea*." *Children's Literature in Education* 11 (May 1973): 58–67.

Frazer, Sir James. *The Golden Bough*. Abridged ed. London: Macmillan, 1963.

Frye, Northrop. *Anatomy of Criticism*. Princeton: Princeton UP, 1957.

Hamilton, Virginia. *The Planet of Junior Brown*. New York: Macmillan, 1971.

Harmon, Elva. Rev. of *A Wizard of Earthsea*. *Library Journal* 94 (15 May 1969): 2104.

Hinton, S. E. *The Outsiders*. New York: Viking, 1967.

——. "Teen-Agers Are for Real." *New York Times Book Review* 27 August 1967: 26–29.

Jago, Wendy. "'A Wizard of Earthsea' and the Charge of Escapism." *Children's Literature in Education* 8 (July 1972): 21–29.

Kroeber, Theodora. *Ishi, Last of His Tribe*. Berkeley: Parnassus Press, 1964.

Kuznets, Lois R. "'High Fantasy' in America: A Study of Lloyd Alexander, Ursula Le Guin, and Susan Cooper." *The Lion and the Unicorn* 9 (1985): 19–35.

Lasseter, Rollin A. "Four Letters about Le Guin." *Ursula K. Le Guin: Voyager to Inner Lands and to Outer Space*. Ed. Joe De Bolt. Literary Criticism Series. Port Washington, NY: Kennikat Press, 1979. 89–114.

Le Guin, Ursula K. "The Child and the Shadow." *Quarterly Journal of The Library of Congress* 32 (April 1975): 139–48.

——. "Dreams Must Explain Themselves." *Algol* 21 (November 1973): 7–10, 12, 14.

——. *The Farthest Shore*. New York: Atheneum, 1972.

——. *From Elfland to Poughkeepsie*. Portland: Pendragon Press, 1973.

——. *The Language of the Night: Essays on Fantasy and Science Fiction*. Ed. Susan Wood. New York: Berkley Books, 1985. G. P. Putnam's, 1979.

——. *The Lathe of Heaven*. New York: Scribner's, 1971.

——. "The Rule of Names." *Fantastic* 13 (April 1964): 79–88.

——. *Tehanu*. New York: Atheneum, 1990.

——. "The Tombs of Atuan." *Worlds of Fantasy* 1 (Winter 1970): 4–76.

——. *The Tombs of Atuan*. New York: Atheneum, 1971.

——. "Why Are Americans Afraid of Dragons?" *Pacific Northwest Library Association Quarterly* 38 (Winter 1974): 14–18.

——. *A Wizard of Earthsea*. Berkeley: Parnassus Press, 1968.

——. "The Word of Unbinding." *Fantastic* 13 (January 1964): 67–73.

Lewis, Naomi. "The Making of a Mage." Rev. of *A Wizard of Earthsea*. *Times Literary Supplement* 2 April 1971: 383.

Manlove, C. N. "Conservatism in the Fantasy of Le Guin." *Extrapolation* 21 (Fall 1980): 287–97.

Molson, Francis J. "The Earthsea Trilogy: Ethical Fantasy for Children." *Ursula K. Le Guin: Voyager to Inner Lands and to Outer Space.* Ed. Joe De Bolt. Literary Criticism Series. Port Washington, NY: Kennikat Press, 1979. 128–49.

Myers, Doris T. "'True Speech' in the Fantasies of Tolkien and Le Guin." *Forum Linguisticum* 7.2 (December 1982): 95–106.

Nicholls, Peter. "Showing Children the Value of Death." Rev. of *The Farthest Shore. Foundation* 5 (January 1974): 71–80.

O'Brien, Robert C. *Mrs. Frisby and the Rats of NIMH.* New York: Macmillan, 1971.

Pfeiffer, John R. "'But Dragons Have Keen Ears': On Hearing 'Earthsea' with Recollections of 'Beowulf.'" *Ursula K. Le Guin: Voyager to Inner Lands and to Outer Space.* Ed. Joe De Bolt. Literary Criticism Series. Port Washington, NY: Kennikat Press, 1979. 115–27.

Rappaport, Karen. Rev. of *The Farthest Shore. The Science Fiction Review Monthly* 9 (November 1975): 15.

Rees, David. *The Marble in the Water: Essays on Contemporary Writers of Fiction for Children and Young Adults.* Boston: Horn Book, 1980.

Remington, Thomas J. "A Time to Live and a Time to Die: Cyclical Renewal in the Earthsea Trilogy." *Extrapolation* 21 (Fall 1980): 278–86.

Scholes, Robert. "The Good Witch of the West." *Hollins Critic* 11 (April 1974): 1–12.

——. *Structural Fabulation: An Essay on Fiction of the Future.* University of Notre Dame Ward-Phillips Lectures in English Language and Literature 7. Notre Dame: U of Notre Dame P, 1975.

Sherman, Cordelia. "The Princess and the Wizard: The Fantasy Worlds of Ursula K. Le Guin and George MacDonald." *Children's Literature Association Quarterly* 12 (Spring 1987): 24–28.

Shippey, T. A. "The Magic Art and the Evolution of Words: Ursula Le Guin's Earthsea Trilogy." *Mosaic* 10 (Winter 1977): 147–63.

Slusser, George Edgar. *The Farthest Shores of Ursula K. Le Guin.* Popular Writers of Today 3. San Bernardino, CA: The Borgo Press, 1976.

Smith, Jennifer Farley. "Despair Pervades Prize Books." *Christian Science Monitor* 2 May 1972: 4.

Spivack, Charlotte. *Ursula K. Le Guin.* Twayne's United States Authors Series 453. Boston: Twayne, 1984.

Tavormina, M. Teresa. "A Gate of Horn and Ivory: Dreaming True and False in Earthsea." *Extrapolation* 29 (Winter 1988): 338–48.

Tolkien, J. R. R. *The Lord of the Rings.* New York: Ballantine, 1965.

Townsend, John Rowe. "Four Myths and Only One Hit." Rev. of *The Tombs of Atuan*. *Guardian* (London) 17 May 1972: 9.

Viguers, Ruth H. Rev. of *A Wizard of Earthsea*. *Horn Book* 45 (February 1969): 59–60.

Walker, Jeanne Murray. "Rites of Passage Today: The Cultural Significance of *A Wizard of Earthsea*." *Mosaic* 13 (Spring/Summer 1980): 179–91.

White, Ted. Rev. of *The Tombs of Atuan*. *Fantastic Science Fiction* 2 (February 1972): 112–13.

White, Virginia L. "Bright the Hawk's Flight: The Journey of the Hero in Ursula Le Guin's Earthsea Trilogy." *Forum* 20 (1979): 34–45.

2: Alien Encounters

S CIENCE FICTION IS URSULA K. LE GUIN'S preferred arena for academic discourse. Not only has she encouraged and supported the establishment of academic organizations devoted to a study of the genre, but she has also maintained an academic presence in this area for more than twenty-five years. She subscribes to the major science fiction journals (and usually reads them), participates on editorial boards of journals devoted to science fiction and/or fantasy, writes occasional scholarly articles, and carries on an academic correspondence with science fiction scholars. She has followed the developments in the field with great interest, as both a creative writer and a scholar, although she insists that she is not qualified to be a scholar and has no interest in becoming one. (I hesitate to agree with her self-assessment in this area, since anyone who came within a stone's throw of completing a Ph.D. in medieval French poetry can hardly be unqualified for scholarship.) In Taoism, which by her own claim she practices inconsistently, calling oneself ignorant is almost a boast, so she is not being self-denigrating when she confesses to academic ignorance. Although she is widely read in feminist literary theory, she steadfastly refuses to read other flavor-of-the-month theorists such as Derrida or Foucault. Nevertheless, having lived her entire life in an academic milieu, she can comfortably encounter critics on their own turf and respond to their remarks in their own language.

Le Guin's earliest science fiction works have mostly escaped the scouring of critics. Between 1962 and 1968 she published five science fiction short stories and three science fiction novels. The stories are "April in Paris," "The Masters," "Darkness Box," "Selection," and "The Dowry of Angyar," all of which were published in *Fantastic* or *Amazing*. Some critics might carp about the classification of a story like "Darkness Box" as science fiction, since it contains a witch, a talking cat, and several mythical creatures, but the early stories are generally lumped together under that generic label. However, since these tales are mostly ignored by scholars, their classification is a moot point.

The three novels receive more attention, although they did not do so when they first appeared. *Rocannon's World* and *Planet of Exile* both appeared in 1966, and *City of Illusions* came out the following year. All were original paperback publications from Ace. In fact, each of the first two was published as one-half of an "Ace Double." An Ace Double was a paperback that contained two entire science fiction novels (or occasionally a collection of short stories) bound together, back to back and upside down. The two novels often had nothing whatsoever in common except their publisher. For science fiction readers, the Ace Double was a wonderful boon: two books for the price of one. And the price was exceptionally reasonable, even by 1966 standards — fifty cents in America, sixty-five cents in Australia. For an author, Ace could be an avenue to a long-denied publication; in fact, Le Guin deliberately turned to science fiction after years of rejection letters because she knew there was a market for readily classifiable works. For Ace, the Double was a guaranteed way to introduce new science fiction writers by binding their novels with those of a known author. *Rocannon's World* was bound with Avram Davidson's *The Kar-Chee Reign*, a sequel which was bound to sell to readers who liked Davidson's earlier Kar-Chee story. *Planet of Exile*'s twin was Thomas M. Disch's *Mankind Under the Leash*. With *City of Illusions* in 1967, Le Guin graduated to Ace singles; her name was beginning to be familiar enough to stand on its own.

The downside of original paperback publication was a lack of reviews. Few review organs look at paperbacks. Four science fiction magazines (*New Worlds, Fantasy and Science Fiction, Australian Science Fiction Review*, and *Analog*) noted the emergence of a new voice in the genre, but only die-hard science fiction fans were likely to see these reviews. The scholarly journals dedicated to science fiction had not yet been founded, except for *Extrapolation*, which was at that time an informal newsletter. The original audience for Le Guin's early novels was thus a closed and limited one. Even when the three books were reissued in hardback by Garland in 1975 they received little critical attention, and even then the attention (and the new editions) were due to Le Guin's so-called overnight success with *The Left Hand of Darkness* in 1969. *The Left Hand of Darkness* was also an original Ace paperback, but it appeared in a hardback edition that same year. While the three earlier novels were well written and inventive, they were traditional representatives of the genre; *The Left Hand of Darkness* was something different.

All four books are set in the distant future, mostly on alien worlds. In Le Guin's projected future, the League of All Worlds — later replaced by the Ekumen — sends individuals to recruit new planetary members or entire groups to seed colonies. *Rocannon's World* deals with the effort of a League ethnographer to save a non-technological planet from invasion by a rebellious League world. In *Planet of Exile*, an abandoned League colony forges links with the native population of the colonized planet, and in *City of Illusions*, a descendant of those colonists comes to Earth to find out what happened to the League. Though set on Earth, the latter book is also about alien encounters: the protagonist himself is an alien, and Earth has been taken over by the alien Shing, who are responsible for the collapse of the League of All Worlds centuries earlier. In this future chronology, *The Left Hand of Darkness* picks up long after the events in the first three books. The Shing have apparently been overcome and there is a new organization of planets called the Ekumen, less exploitative and high-handed than the League had been.

The Left Hand of Darkness is set on the planet Gethen, which the Ekumen exploration team has called "Winter" — an accurate description of the planet's climate. A stuffy young Earth male named Genly Ai has been sent to Gethen to persuade its inhabitants to join the Ekumen. His efforts are hampered by disbelief among Gethenians, who have never seen an alien, by political machinations, and by Ai's own inability to deal with the climate and with the biological peculiarity of the Gethenians: they are androgynous. The story has two protagonists, Genly Ai and Estraven, his only Gethenian supporter. Much of the plot deals with their slow attempts to forge a relationship in order to bring about the desired goal of membership in the Ekumen. The presence of a planet populated by androgynes is not the only striking feature of the book: the structure too is unusual. Constructed of bits and pieces of different kinds of documents, the form of the book is distinctly post-modern. Some of the chapters are Genly Ai's first-person narration, some are first-person entries from Estraven's journal, and others are straightforward retellings of Gethenian myths and legends or excerpts from official Ekumen documents.

The Left Hand of Darkness stunned the science fiction critics. Not only did it win the Nebula Award for best novel of 1969, given by the Science Fiction Writers of America, but it also won the popularity contest known as the Hugo Award, given by science fiction fans, whose critical acumen is often as astute as that of the professional writers. Walker Publishing issued two different hardback editions (one for the Science Fiction Book Club) in 1969, the same year as the original Ace paperback. In 1994 Walker brought out a special 25th Anniversary Edition. *The Left Hand of Darkness* is one of the seminal texts of science fiction, as important and influential as Mary Shelley's *Frankenstein* (1818), which is often cited as the first science fiction novel. *Left Hand* is one of the three main foci of Le Guin criticism; the other two are Earthsea and utopian literature. Most of the scholarly commentary on Le Guin's early science fiction revolves around *Left Hand*. Even when scholars were writing about her previous novels, they used *Left Hand* as a touchstone. Two of Le Guin's later science fiction novels, *The Dispossessed* and *Always Coming Home*, are also considered major works in the genre, but they actually fit better into the category of utopian literature.

When Le Guin's fourth science fiction novel first appeared, it did not garner completely favorable reviews. A book as startling as *The Left Hand of Darkness* is bound to provoke both negative and positive responses. Alexei Panshin, reviewing the novel for *Fantasy and Science Fiction*, judged it "a flat failure" (50). Panshin was also the first reviewer to object to Le Guin's use of masculine pronouns in reference to the androgynes. The feminists who were just beginning to enter the science fiction field were disappointed because Le Guin did not go far enough in her examination of gender. Joanna Russ, a feminist scholar and science fiction writer, wanted a more thorough exploration of gender roles on Gethen; who, for instance, takes care of the children? In a 1970 article, "The Image of Women in Science Fiction," Russ reluctantly admits that the masculine pronouns are required by the limitations of the English language, but she complains that everything else in the novel is masculine as well.

Other reviewers praised the novel for its insight and originality. In a literary survey for *Nebula Award Stories 5*, Darko Suvin, one of the earliest recognized scholars of science fiction, had no hesitation in calling it the "most memorable novel of the year" (203). The controversy over the masculine presentation of the Gethenians did not interfere with the book's popularity and, in fact, may have contributed to its fame. The majority of science fiction writers and readers agreed with Suvin's assessment, as is evidenced by *Left Hand* being voted the best book of the year by both writers and fans.

The controversy over *Left Hand* never died down completely. It was stirred up again in 1971 when the Australian science fiction magazine *SF Commentary* published an article by Polish writer Stanislaw Lem (as translated from German by Franz Rottensteiner). "Lost Opportunities," the English title, was a critical assessment of *The Left Hand of Darkness*, with the emphasis on "critical." Lem finds the novel psychologically unsound because the Gethenians' constant gender changes should wreak havoc on relationships and personal identity. He deplores Le Guin's failure to pursue such possibilities, and he also accuses her of presenting the Gethenians as wholly masculine in behavior, dress, and speech. Le Guin responded in a letter to the editor of *SF Commentary* several months later, inviting Lem to write the novel he proposes hers should have been and explaining that Lem has misinterpreted the physiology of the Gethenians. He has overlooked the mechanisms by which long-term relationships could exist on Gethen. Le Guin also addresses the question of masculinity. She says she did consider inventing a neutral pronoun but could not find a way to make it work. One reason why readers sometimes jump to the conclusion that the Gethenians are almost wholly masculine, Le Guin suggests, is that the readers are reacting to their own culturally conditioned assumptions that a woman could not be a prime minister or pull a loaded sled across the ice and that trousers are an inherently masculine form of clothing. Since Gethen is an extremely cold planet, all the inhabitants wear tunics and trousers; the choice of clothing has nothing to do with gender. How could unisex clothing be considered masculine?

In this letter Le Guin was still able to respond with patience and good humor, but the continued attacks on her androgynes would eventually bring her temper to boiling point. Her most public defense of *The Left Hand of Darkness* appeared in 1976 in an essay for a feminist collection, *Aurora: Beyond Equality*. Le Guin's essay posed the question "Is Gender Necessary?" Identifying herself as a feminist, the author explains the process by which she decided to strip her Gethenians of gender in order to see the basic components of humanity — what men and women have in common beneath their sexual differences. This fictional experiment was, in a sense, a side issue for Le Guin, who contends that the book is really about fidelity and betrayal. But the essay explores the side issue in detail. The only regrets Le Guin admits to are a failure to invent a new form of government for the Gethenians, a failure to explore fully the psychological implications of Gethenian physiology (which seems to be a concession to Lem's earlier criticism), and a failure to show the androgynes in roles our culture deems "feminine." Although this last regret is listed as the author's failure, it is also an implicit criticism of her audience's inability to see beyond their own cultural conditioning — to imagine a woman, or a man/woman, performing tasks we traditionally associate with the male.

Seven years of irritation surface in Le Guin's defense of her use of pronouns. Discussing the frequent criticism that her Gethenians seem to be male, she states: "This rises in part from the choice of pronoun. I call Gethenians 'he,' because I utterly refuse to mangle English by inventing a pronoun for 'he/she.' 'He' is the generic pronoun, damn it, in English" (*Language* 168).

The need to defend her work, particularly to her fellow feminists, brought Le Guin face to face with the modern issues exercising feminist thought, particularly with the way language reflects and constructs cultural beliefs. As a result of this controversy, Le Guin began to explore these issues more deeply, to question her own assumptions and those of society, and to read the works of feminist literary theorists. This was a first step down a road that would change her literary direction completely. The changes are clearly rung in a revised version of "Is Gender Necessary?" When Le Guin updated her first essay collection, *The Language of the Night*, for British publication in 1989, she took herself to task for her earlier feminist failures, singling out "Is Gender Necessary?" for its inadequacies:

This 1976 piece has been quoted from a great deal, often to my intense embarrassment. Within a few years I came to disagree completely with some of the things I said in it, but there they were in print, and all I could do was writhe in deserved misery as the feminists told me off and the masculinists patted my head. Clearly it would have been unethical to rewrite the 1976 text, to disappear it; so it appears here, complete, but with remarks and annotations and self-recriminations from later years. I do hope I don't have to do this again in the nineties.

(*Language*, Revised edition 2)

The revised essay, called "Is Gender Necessary? Redux," is printed in two columns, with the 1976 text on the left and Le Guin's 1988 comments in italics in the right column. (The symbolism of this placement could not have escaped her, and it must have been deliberate, since the first appearance of the revised essay in *Dancing at the Edge of the World* in 1989 simply uses bracketed italics to incorporate the new comments.) One of the first changes is an admission that androgyny was not the side issue she had wished to relegate it to in her earlier remarks, but that it is in fact central to almost everything in the book. Trying to place it on the sidelines was a defensive measure; the author had been feeling extremely defensive at the time she wrote the article because of the constant attacks on *Left Hand*. Le Guin also apologizes for her own cultural assumptions, which led her to make heterosexual behavior the norm on Gethen and to accept "he" unquestioningly as the generic pronoun. Instead of criticizing the cultural conditioning of her readers, she should have been looking a bit closer at her own conditioning. Her final assessment of *The Left Hand of Darkness* is an apology to feminists:

> Men were inclined to be satisfied with the book, which allowed them a safe trip into androgyny and back, from a conventionally male viewpoint. But many women wanted it to go further, to dare more, to explore androgyny from a woman's point of view as well as a man's . . . . I think women were justified in asking more courage of me and a more rigorous thinking-through of implications. (*Language*, Revised edition 171)

The intervening years between "Is Gender Necessary?" and "Is Gender Necessary? Redux" abounded in critical discussion of Le Guin's science fiction novels, which by 1988 were considerable in number. As each new novel changed the corpus of her works, critics responded by altering their own perceptions. By far the most criticism concentrated on *The Left Hand of Darkness*; however, before the main scholarly advance on that novel began, several other science fiction works appeared.

In 1969, the same year *Left Hand* was published, one of Le Guin's most anthologized stories, "Nine Lives," made its initial appearance. It was her first big sale outside of the standard science fiction market, appearing in the November issue of *Playboy* and proving the worth of her new agent, Virginia Kidd. Kidd's aggressive representation is largely responsible for placing Le Guin's short stories in mainstream (that is, non-science fiction) publications and for getting lucrative book contracts with important publishers. Thanks to Kidd, Le Guin would no longer have to accept original paperback publication of any of her books except her occasional self-published chapbooks.

The first appearance of "Nine Lives" also represents the only occasion on which Le Guin encountered explicit gender prejudice as a science fiction writer. *Playboy* insisted on presenting the author as "U. K. Le Guin," fearing that readers would not accept a science fiction story written by a woman. Science fiction was perceived as a masculine genre that appealed specifically to adolescent males, and for many years women writers had resorted to pseudonyms and initials in order to get their work published. Realizing this, Le Guin submitted the story under her initials. At the time Le Guin was mildly amused; not until much later did she realize that as a feminist she should have been offended by the need to hide her gender. For Le Guin, it was enough that she had broken through into mainstream publication: her work would find a wider audience in *Playboy*, and she would receive a larger paycheck. Writing was, after all, her business as well as her vocation.

Other than reviews, Le Guin's science fiction did not receive even casual critical attention until 1972, by which time she had published three more important works of science fiction: another novel, *The Lathe of Heaven* (1971), and two novellas, "Vaster Than Empires and More Slow" (1971) and "The Word for World Is Forest" (1972). (Novellas have remained a popular literary form in science fiction, although this hybrid between a novel and a short story has fallen out of use in other genres.) *The Lathe of Heaven* was a departure for Le Guin in that it was not set in the universe of her previous science fiction, which was unified by the presence of an alien race called the Hain, who seeded life on all the other planets in the universe, including Earth. *Lathe* is set on the Pacific coast in the near future and tells the story of George Orr, whose dreams have the remarkable ability to change reality. The anonymous reviewer in the *Times Literary Supplement* ("Myths of Anti-Climax") found *Lathe* unconvincing, but fellow writer Theodore Sturgeon, reviewing the book for the *New York Times Book Review*, praised Le Guin as a writer's writer who has written "a rare and powerful synthesis of poetry and science, reason and emotion" (33).

The two novellas are set in the Hainish universe. "Vaster Than Empires and More Slow," which appeared in the original science fiction anthology *New Dimensions I*, relates the story of a survey team on a planet populated by a single vegetative intelligence. "The Word for World Is Forest" was Le Guin's contribution to Harlan Ellison's much anticipated anthology *Again, Dangerous Visions*, a collection of original stories meant to be daring and different, as befitted writers coming to be known as science fiction's "New Left." To modern readers many of the stories in this collection seem brutally misogynistic, but in 1972 the New Left was more interested in literary experimentation and sexual frankness than in changing the way women were represented in science fiction. Feminism was not yet a force in science fiction. Le Guin's story, strongly influenced by her pacifism and her negative views on the Vietnam War, castigates Earth explorers for razing the living trees of another planet and forcing the natives into slavery. Both stories received considerable attention from critics in the 1970s and eighties.

The first minor critical appraisal of Le Guin's science fiction appeared in 1972 in *Extrapolation*, one of the new science fiction journals. In an article entitled "Virgin Territory: Women and Sex in Science Fiction," Beverly Friend mentions *Left Hand* as an exemplum of the correct way to represent gender differences. Friend covers too many disparate novels to contribute any real insights into Le Guin's work, but this is one of the first of many occasions when Le Guin would be cited in articles dealing with science fiction in general. By the end of the 1970s no reputable critic could write about twentieth-century developments in science fiction without at least mentioning Le Guin.

The first in-depth scholarly discussion of a Le Guin work was Douglas Barbour's 1973 article, "*The Lathe of Heaven*: Taoist Dream," in *Algol*, a science fiction fan magazine. *Algol's* November issue contained a special Le Guin section, which included Barbour's article, an interview with the author, Le Guin's article "Dreams Must Explain Themselves," her Earthsea story "The Rule of Names," and a portion of her National Book Award acceptance speech for *The Farthest Shore*. Barbour's article is noteworthy as being the first to examine the influence of Taoism on Le Guin's work. Barbour became rather a one-note musician in the 1970s, writing articles about Taoist influence on Earthsea, on the early Hainish novels, and on *The Dispossessed*, as well as on *The Lathe of Heaven*, culminating in his 1976 Ph.D. dissertation, "Patterns and Meaning in the Novels of Ursula K. Le Guin, Joanna Russ and Samuel R. Delany, 1962–1972."

As the first critic to give Le Guin's work concentrated attention, Barbour was the first to point out influences and connections that have long since become givens in Le Guin criticism: her use of Taoism and balanced dualism, particularly the dualistic imagery of dark and light. Barbour also coined the phrase "Hainish universe" to describe most of her science fiction; the Hainish origins of her planets might otherwise have remained a minor background note to the novels. In a 1974 article, "Wholeness and Balance in the Hainish Novels of Ursula K. Le Guin," Barbour is the first critic to note that Le Guin's interplay of opposites can be seen as a dance: "This dance of shadows and light is the proper image for their interplay in all Le Guin's work: both the light and the dark are necessary if any pattern is to emerge from chaos" (165). This article traces the dark and light imagery through *Rocannon's World, Planet of Exile, City of Illusions, The Left Hand of Darkness*, and "The Word for World Is Forest." For Barbour, the images are explicitly related to Taoism, since for Taoists a perfect balance of darkness and light is necessary for wholeness.

Taken together, Barbour's articles provide a holistic context for Le Guin's works, including the Earthsea books; all the works are connected through Le Guin's use of Taoism and dualism. But other critics were slow to build on the connections. None of Barbour's comments was inflammatory or controversial in the least; his attitude toward Le Guin was one of respectful worship. It would require a more combative critical approach to provoke further serious criticism of Le Guin's science fiction, and that combative approach appeared in one of the first critical monographs on the genre, David Ketterer's *New Worlds for Old: The Apocalyptic Imagination, Science Fiction, and American Literature*, published by Indiana University Press in 1974.

The thesis of Ketterer's book is that science fiction is concerned with apocalyptic transformations — large-scale destruction followed by creation of entire worlds. Ketterer considers the Apocalypse to be the basic myth on which all science fiction is built. He chooses *The Left Hand of Darkness* for a lengthy discussion of what happens when a science fiction book is overdependent on its underlying mythic structure. Building on Northrop Frye's theories, Ketterer states that the "mythic basis of any fiction . . . should exist irrespective of an author's intentions and in a severely displaced relationship to the story line" (77). According to Ketterer, this is exactly what Le Guin fails to do: her plot is subordinate to the underlying myth of death and rebirth, and the novel is therefore a failure as science fiction. Like many critics, Ketterer singles out the androgyny as a problem:

> That an "intelligible" summary of the often arbitrary action of Le Guin's novel is possible without any mention of what it is that makes the Gethenians especially distinctive, especially alien — namely their unique form of bisexuality — argues against the book's structural integrity.
>
> (*New Worlds* 79–80)

Structural integrity would demand that androgyny be a vital part of the surface plot. Instead, it is clearly part of the underlying mythic structure.

The importance of Ketterer's remarks lies not so much in his interpretation of *Left Hand* as in the response he provoked from other science fiction critics. His book was the focus of a session of the 1974 Science Fiction Research Association conference. Selections from the papers read at that session were published in the second volume of the new journal *Science-Fiction Studies* in 1975. One of the papers is by Le Guin herself, responding to Ketterer's criticism of *Left Hand*. Le Guin's basic defense is that she and Ketterer have different definitions for the terms myth and symbol. She aligns herself with Jung, whereas Ketterer aligns himself with Frye; in *Left Hand* she was dealing with archetypes, not with intellectual constructs. Moreover, she claims that her novel has nothing whatsoever to do with the apocalyptic transformations Ketterer is interested in. It is clear from her comments that she associates anything apocalyptic with the Christian Apocalypse, the final battle at the end of the world described in the Book of Revelation, in which she has neither belief nor interest. Her remarks are highly critical of Ketterer, as indeed were the papers of the other presenters at the SFRA session.

Science-Fiction Studies allowed Ketterer the opportunity to reply to his accusers (as did the SFRA panel), so he has the final word. The panel has misunderstood his book, he claims, then he turns to a restatement of his basic thesis and theory of literature. He stresses that by the term "apocalyptic literature" he does not mean "Apocalyptic literature" in the biblical sense. Responding to Le Guin's remarks, he suggests that she hasn't actually read his book, states that he knows perfectly well what "myth" and "symbol" mean, and stands behind his assessment of *Left Hand* as an admirable but "radically flawed" book (145). A reader familiar with both *Left Hand* and *New Worlds for Old* can't help concluding that neither author has much understanding of the other.

The Ketterer controversy no doubt stimulated the idea of producing a special issue of *Science-Fiction Studies* devoted to Le Guin later in the year. The November 1975 issue, guest edited by science fiction critic Darko Suvin, comprised twelve articles about Le Guin's science fiction. Suvin considered the issue incomplete because it lacked any articles that would incorporate Le Guin's Earthsea books with her science fiction. Suvin's remark about Earthsea contains two important implications: 1) that the science fiction community felt a sense of ownership in Le Guin's entire corpus of work and 2) that science fiction critics had no scholarly interest in Le Guin's fantasy. The territorial feeling would later lead to insecurity when the science fiction community began to suspect Le Guin of wanting to jump ship, so to speak — to abandon science fiction for the more reputable and remunerable field of mainstream literature, as Kurt Vonnegut had done quite noisily years earlier. The second implication resulted in

a reluctant sense of duty among Le Guin's science fiction critics, who began to include obligatory comments about Earthsea in their articles.

Le Guin's high esteem among the science fiction critics was already
established by the time *Science-Fiction Studies* brought out its special issue.
Scholarly conferences featured special sessions on her work, and she was
regularly invited to be a guest speaker at academic gatherings. *The Left
Hand of Darkness* had won both of the major science fiction awards, the
Hugo Award and the Nebula Award. Her most recent novel, *The Dispossessed* (1974), had also won both awards. Two stories, "The Ones Who
Walk Away from Omelas" and "The Word for World Is Forest," had won
Hugos, and a third story, "The Day Before the Revolution," had won a
Nebula. As the first woman to have won the Hugo and Nebula for best
novel and the only writer to have won both awards twice, Le Guin was a
major figure in science fiction and a suitable focus for a single-author issue
of the new journal.

Several of the articles in the special issue centered on Le Guin's early
works. One of the most discerning pieces is Rafail Nudelman's "An Approach to the Structure of Le Guin's SF." (In the science fiction community, "SF" is the standard shorthand for "science fiction.") Nudelman's
premise is that Le Guin's early novels share a parallel structure on multiple
levels. Nudelman sees a one-to-one correspondence at three levels: that of
the universal, involving the far-flung members of the League of All
Worlds, each world separated from the others by space and time; the
planetary level, at which isolated pockets of settlement divided by huge icy
wastes (or unending wild forest) reflect the isolation of the scattered planets in space; the personal level, at which individuals are equally isolated in
space and time. Nudelman compares this multi-leveled structure to a piece
of music that expresses its theme through variations. At all of the levels the
fragments are yearning for oneness, so the movement in the novels is from
fragmentation to unity. But this is not a closed system in which fragmentation circles through unity and then back to its original state; both the
planet and the individual are changed in some way, so that the motion in
Le Guin's novels is actually spiral rather than circular. Each book represents this motion as a journey that is both physical and psychological, spiraling upward. The spiral structure is an important element in Le Guin
criticism; many other critics have also noticed it, either on their own or
through reading an article like Nudelman's or Le Guin's own "Dreams
Must Explain Themselves."

Another article in the 1975 special issue is significant in that it points
out a central metaphor in Le Guin's early science fiction. The title of the
article says it all: "The Forest as Metaphor for Mind: 'The Word for
World Is Forest' and 'Vaster Than Empires and More Slow.'" Ian Wat-

son, the author of the article, propounds the notion that Le Guin's planet-wide forests are a metaphor for Jung's collective unconscious. The two novellas Watson discusses use the metaphor in different ways, but they are connected by this shared metaphor, by allusions to Andrew Marvell's poetry, and by a concern with the relationship between dreams and reality. Although the bulk of the article shows no deep insight into the stories, Watson rightly asserts that the forest metaphor is an important aspect of Le Guin's work.

"Public and Private Imperatives in Le Guin's Novels" was John Huntington's contribution to the special issue of *Science-Fiction Studies.* Huntington notices that Le Guin's heroes are usually professional or amateur anthropologists who face a conflict between public duty to their own culture and private duty toward individuals in the culture in which they find themselves. The hero is inevitably forced to take public action that comes at a high personal cost — generally the sacrifice of a friend. Rather than moving toward unity between opposites, as other critics have claimed, Le Guin explores the tension between opposites that yearn for a unity they cannot ever attain. Huntington says that the tension between public values and private values is best expressed in *The Left Hand of Darkness,* in which Genly Ai's public duty to bring Gethen into the Ekumen (descendant of the League of All Worlds) both conflicts with and balances his private duty to his friend Estraven. Huntington also points out that whereas Le Guin initially viewed a kind of primitive economic feudalism as the only alternative to imperialism, in her more recent works (recent as of 1975) she seems to be examining more modern political systems as possible alternatives.

Another article in the special issue also explored Le Guin's developing politics, David L. Porter's "The Politics of Le Guin's Opus." Porter sees that development in three stages: an early existentialism, followed by Taoism, then by anarchism. This represents a movement from extreme individualism toward social responsibility. Porter adds to the "balance of opposites" approach to Le Guin's work by claiming that it is not balance but interdependence that is the key. Le Guin's opposites need each other to maintain existence. According to Porter, Le Guin's first phase, existentialism, is represented by the main characters in *Planet of Exile,* Jakob and Rolery, who risk the destruction of both their peoples by engaging in a forbidden love affair. The second phase of Taoism can be seen in *A Wizard of Earthsea, The Left Hand of Darkness,* and *The Lathe of Heaven.* Anarchism is most apparent in "The Word for World Is Forest" and *The Dispossessed.*

Le Guin's work, says Porter, is about the contemporary world — about imperialism and all the other -isms of interest to radical American intellectuals. Le Guin is a political activist who must be taken seriously. Her work critiques contemporary politics and offers alternatives. A realistic mode of writing is not necessarily the best means of portraying the realities of our existence, as Le Guin proves in her science fiction. While Porter's points are perceptive and well argued, I cannot help suspecting him of having an ulterior motive — trying to raise science fiction into literary respectability by making it relevant to modern politics. Many early science fiction scholars, academics seeking validation of their work, shared just such an agenda, as is easily understandable. Since Le Guin's novels were extremely well written and made use of complex literary strategies and philosophical concepts, they were ideal examples for the apologists, who were, at least in America, fighting a long-standing tradition of pulp science fiction abounding in stereotypical bug-eyed monsters, mad scientists, action heroes armed with blasters, and blonde bimbos in need of much rescuing.

George Slusser's 1976 pamphlet on Le Guin was the first sustained criticism of her work. I have already discussed Slusser's contribution to Earthsea criticism. He had even more to say about her science fiction. *The Farthest Shores of Ursula K. Le Guin* objects to several of the approaches in the Le Guin issue of *Science-Fiction Studies*, in particular the Porter article. Far from being an interlude in Le Guin's political development, claims Slusser, Taoism "is and has always been the strongest single force behind her work" (3). Slusser also disagrees with critics who want to read Le Guin's polarities as an attempt to reach a synthesis of opposites. Nor is Le Guin's universe open-ended, as Nudelman would have it; the pattern remains the same.

Having listed his objections to the previous criticism, Slusser provides his own interpretation of everything Le Guin had written up to that point. He sees her emphasis shifting from external to internal issues, from a celebration of balance to a concern with the problems inherent in maintaining a balance, and from a conventional storytelling technique to different ways of experimenting with point of view. Le Guin's first three science fiction novels deal with opposite principles Slusser terms "elusiveness of control" and "fortunate paradox," although what he means by those terms is never completely clear. By elusiveness of control he apparently means that what seems to be a right choice to a protagonist is really a wrong one; by fortunate paradox he seems to be referring to the unpredictable twists that change the protagonist's perception. Slusser also says that Le Guin uses binding symbols in these first three books — physical objects that represent balance, such as the jewel in *Rocannon's World* and patterning frames in *City of Illusions*.

For Slusser, as for many others, *The Left Hand of Darkness* is the apogee of Le Guin's work. One of his questions about this novel is why an enlightened galactic confederation like the Ekumen seems so blind to the approaching war on Gethen. The long history of the Ekumen and the League of All Worlds contains many parallel situations, so the Ekumen's representatives ought to be able to predict what is unfolding. Slusser suggests that the unusual sexuality of the Gethenians is too large a barrier to understanding for the off-worlders to notice political developments. But Genly Ai *has* noticed developments, though he dismisses or misinterprets them. He thinks a petty border skirmish between two alien nations is too unimportant to bother with in light of the planet-wide significance of his mission. Slusser either fails to notice this or thinks it insignificant, but it is part of the characterization of Genly Ai as a slightly pompous and self-important young man.

One of Slusser's comments about *Left Hand* points out an important theme that runs throughout all of Le Guin's works: "The theme of roots and rootlessness is central to Le Guin's work" (21). This theme has grown from novel to novel. All her protagonists have been rootless in some fashion, but in her later novels she pins this notion to actual roots, as in "The Word for World Is Forest." Roots and dreams become the same thing.

Slusser's pamphlet contains the best discussion of *shifgrethor* I have seen in the criticism. "Shifgrethor" is a word coined by Le Guin to describe the system of status on Gethen. As Slusser explains the term, "This status is not rank, but its opposite, the ability to maintain equality in any relationship, and to do so by respecting the person of the other" (23). Slusser explains how shifgrethor interferes with the initial relationship between Estraven and Genly Ai. Ai does not understand shifgrethor nor how it affects all relationships on Gethen. Like the naive narrator in ancient travel literature, the visitor from afar who has to have everything explained to him in detail, Genly is educated step by step.

Most of Slusser's pamphlet is a general introduction to Le Guin's works. *The Farthest Shores of Ursula K. Le Guin* is often cited by science fiction scholars, but it has had no impact outside the genre. As much as Slusser and other science fiction critics yearned to bring their field into academic respectability, it was a scholar from outside science fiction who succeeded in bringing Le Guin criticism into the mainstream. In 1974 Robert Scholes, Ward-Phillips lecturer in English language and literature at Notre Dame, chose to devote his four lectures to a genre he christened "structural fabulation," by which he really meant science fiction. The first three lectures established his theories about science fiction's role in contemporary literature, arguing that it deserved serious attention from critics, and his final lecture focused entirely on the work of one science fiction writer in an attempt to apply his literary theories to actual literature. The science fiction writer he chose was, of course, Le Guin. This fourth lecture was published in *Hollins Critic* in 1974, and it later became the fourth chapter of the book based on the lectures, *Structural Fabulation: An Essay on Fiction of the Future*, published by the University of Notre Dame Press in 1975.

Science fiction critics agree that Scholes's essay on Le Guin, "The Good Witch of the West," single-handedly thrust her work into national prominence among academics. Suddenly Le Guin was a major contemporary American writer. Nowadays most literary scholars are aware of her status in American letters even though some of them remain unaware that she writes science fiction. She has become a "name" in contemporary literature, and no anthology of American literature is complete without at least one of her short stories. Although Le Guin might have eventually attained these heights without any help from Scholes, his critical attention certainly served to give her a leg up.

According to Scholes, Le Guin is the one writer who can successfully combine all the ingredients necessary for successful science fiction: "[I]f I were to choose one writer to illustrate the way in which it is possible to unite speculation and fabulation in works of compelling power and beauty, employing a language that is fully adequate to this esthetic intention, that writer would be the Good Witch of the West" (*Structural Fabulation* 79). He adopts this affectionate title for Le Guin as a tribute to the Oz books and a reference to Le Guin's location on the Oregon coast, thus linking science fiction and children's literature in a way no science fiction scholar would have done in 1974.

Scholes is explicit about his regard for Le Guin's work: "She is probably the best writer of speculative fabulation working in this country today, and she deserves a place among our major contemporary writers of fiction" (80). The two books Scholes finds most worthy are *A Wizard of Earthsea* and *The Left Hand of Darkness*. After comparing the first to C. S. Lewis's highly acclaimed Narnia books (to Le Guin's advantage), Scholes goes on to discuss *Left Hand*, which he considers her best work. He implicitly dismisses the notion that science fiction is mere escapism:

> In her most mature work, Ursula Le Guin shows us how speculative fabulation can deal with the social dimensions of existence as adequately as the most "realistic" of traditional models — or perhaps more adequately in some important respects. For she does not present us with the details of a social chronicle but raises questions about the nature of social organization itself. She is not so much a sociologist as a structural an-

thropologist, dealing with the principles rather than the data of social organization. (*Structural Fabulation* 87)

Although Scholes's discussion of Le Guin's work does not appear particularly insightful to a reader familiar with the science fiction criticism or the children's literature criticism, it did an inestimable service for Le Guin's reputation and indeed for that of the entire field of science fiction. A major literary critic, author of *The Nature of Narrative* and *Structuralism in Literature*, was acknowledging that science fiction was worthy of study and that Le Guin was worthy of a place among the literary elite. Scholes's assessment, while gratifying to Le Guin, eventually gave rise to some alarm in the science fiction community, where insecurity flourished: if Le Guin is that good, surely she will abandon the science fiction ghetto for life in the literary stratosphere. This fear became an oft-quoted prediction that has dogged Le Guin ever since.

After the 1975 Le Guin issue of *Science-Fiction Studies*, occasional articles on Le Guin continued to pop up in *Science-Fiction Studies*, *Extrapolation*, and *Foundation*, the three leading scholarly journals in science fiction. Many articles ploughed old ground: new scholars kept making the same amazing discoveries others had made previously, finding that Le Guin's works have a spiral structure, that she uses recurring themes and images (particularly androgyny and shadows), that Taoism and feminism influence her work, and that she is a much better writer than the majority of science fiction writers. The authors of these articles seldom show familiarity with previous criticism, but sloppy research is a malady that often infects scholarship in all disciplines, not just science fiction.

In 1977 *Science-Fiction Studies* published an article by Martin Bickman that was more probing than most, "Le Guin's *The Left Hand of Darkness*: Form and Content." The article addresses several issues of interest. Initial reviewers of *Left Hand* had sometimes been confused by the structure of the book, a seemingly random collection of first person narrative, journal entries, reports, and myths. Bickman tries to show that Genly Ai, as the structuring consciousness of the book, selects texts that reflect the process by which he has achieved his own enlightened understanding of Gethen. This allows the reader to share Genly's growth process. Bickman states, "As with much modern literature, then, the complex patterning of the book is not so much a way to tell a story as it is the story itself" (54). Bickman also claims that "the novel achieves unity not in spite of, but because of its variety of voices and perspectives — different angles of vision that create a certain dimensionality and heft" (54). Bickman sees the novel as following a structure based on the familiar Hegelian formula: thesis-antithesis-synthesis. He also applauds Le Guin for stressing the multiplicity of reality by showing the interdependence of myth and fact. Unlike many science fiction writers, most of whom find balancing form and content difficult, Le Guin makes effective use of this duality as well as of the many other sets of opposites scholars have traced in her work.

The wealth of criticism that exploded in the late 1970s included several articles devoted to Le Guin's early science fiction works. Three of the articles in the Olander and Greenberg 1979 collection, *Ursula K. Le Guin*, are of note: Sneja Gunew's "Mythic Reversals: The Evolution of the Shadow Motif," N. B. Hayles's "Androgyny, Ambivalence, and Assimilation in *The Left Hand of Darkness*," and Thomas J. Remington's "The Other Side of Suffering: Touch as Theme and Metaphor in Le Guin's Science Fiction Novels." Gunew's article is noteworthy only for pointing out that Le Guin uses shadow images throughout her work, not only in *A Wizard of Earthsea*. The meanings Gunew assigns to the shadow images are arbitrary and confusing, but it is interesting to see how prevalent that imagery is in the early science fiction novels.

The Hayles article offers more depth of analysis. Hayles provides the reader with a brief history of androgyny, from androgyny as a "lost primordial unity" in ancient cosmogonies (98) to the androgyne as the alien Other. His knowledge of the history allows him particular insight into Le Guin's use of androgyny:

> Thus, androgyny, as it is found in myth, legend, and history, is basically ambivalent; it can be seen either as the augmentation and completion of the self or as a form of self-annihilation, the intrusion of the alien into the self. Whether she was aware of these specific traditions or not, Le Guin uses the ambisexuality of the Gethenians in a remarkably similar way. On one hand, the peculiar Gethenian sexuality can be threatening, a representation of that which is disturbingly alien, while on the other hand, it can stand as a symbol of the wholeness to which man can aspire but only metaphorically attain — a lost state of perfection. (99)

The bulk of Hayles's article is a close reading of *The Left Hand of Darkness* in which he extracts details to prove his thesis. Along the way, he makes several interesting observations. One is that whereas male science fiction writers express the drive toward inclusion by expanding the action in a novel, a woman writer such as Le Guin will instead contract the action to the level of personal relationship. His other observation is specific to Le Guin: she never presents one idea as the whole truth, but instead tries to show through statements and counterstatements that all truths are partial and are subject to change. Le Guin presents all ideas in terms of ambivalence, not just the concept of androgyny.

Like Gunew's essay, the third significant article in the Olander and Greenberg collection is based on a single insight. In this case Thomas Remington has noticed that Le Guin uses touch frequently in her novels.

Although he can't decide whether touch is a theme, an image, or both, he conscientiously collects every instance of touching (both physical and mental) in *Rocannon's World*, *Planet of Exile*, *City of Illusions*, *The Left Hand of Darkness*, *The Lathe of Heaven*, and *The Dispossessed*. Remington shows how touching involves both pain and love in these novels. Touch, particularly a touch between two unlike beings, is the point of contact and of unity; touch is always temporary, yet it creates lasting change in the individual and his or her society.

The other major essay collection of 1979, Joe De Bolt's *Ursula K. Le Guin: Voyager to Inner Lands and to Outer Space*, contains only two articles of significance related to Le Guin's early science fiction. "Solitary Being: The Hero as Anthropologist" builds on the observation made by John Huntington and others that Le Guin's main characters tend to be anthropologists, or more specifically, participant-observers. In this article Karen Sinclair contributes further insight into the observation through her own reading of anthropology and sociology. Le Guin's heroes, Sinclair claims, are social anthropologists. This kind of hero operates as both cultural translator and social commentator. His main purpose is to gather knowledge, and by standing on the threshold between two different cultures, to try (and usually fail) to explain each culture to the other. Such a character is, of necessity, marginal. Although Sinclair's article is not the best exploration of the hero as anthropologist, her comments predate articles by scholars who have a more thorough knowledge of anthropology.

The other useful article in the De Bolt collection is Peter T. Koper's "Science and Rhetoric in the Fiction of Ursula Le Guin." Koper is intrigued by how the language and mindset of science conditions modern ways of thinking, and he claims that Le Guin's works all include strong statements about science "as a mental outlook both powerfully attractive and dangerous" (67). Even the magic in the Earthsea books is really a metaphor for the scientific method. Our modern society has been conditioned to value scientific, verifiable fact over more intuitive ways of knowing, and Le Guin wishes to criticize this outlook as unnecessarily limiting.

Koper applies rhetorical criticism of an Aristotelian cast to his examination of a dozen works: "The Masters," "April in Paris," *The Left Hand of Darkness*, *Rocannon's World*, *Planet of Exile*, *City of Illusions*, *The Lathe of Heaven*, *The Dispossessed*, *A Wizard of Earthsea*, "The Word for World Is Forest," "Vaster Than Empires and More Slow," and "The Ones Who Walk Away from Omelas." These are far too many works to try to discuss in one article, but Koper hopes to prove that all of them are unified by Le Guin's criticism of a reductive scientific outlook on life. By looking closely at the main characters in these works, he tries to show how a scientific outlook alienates the individual from society and from self because of its emphasis on empirical data. All of Le Guin's heroes operate from such a scientific mindset, but they are all also searching for a way to reconnect to the missing parts of their lives — their individuality and their role in society.

By including two fantasy works in his discussion ("April in Paris" and *A Wizard of Earthsea*), Koper claims to be meeting the challenge raised by Darko Suvin in *Science-Fiction Studies*' special issue on Le Guin — to integrate Le Guin's fantasy into the discussion of her science fiction. Koper states that the author's fantasy and science fiction exhibit differences of setting and type of action, but are innately unified by her critique of the scientific method: "What is essential is the argument which runs through most of her major pieces, the way in which explicitly in her science fiction and implicitly in her fantasy, she examines the effects of science on individual personalities" (69).

Jeanne Murray Walker, whose anthropological knowledge contributed original insights into *A Wizard of Earthsea*, also applied her knowledge to Le Guin's science fiction. One of Walker's articles came out in the July 1979 issue of *Science-Fiction Studies*. Because of the time lapse built in to most academic publications, it is impossible to know whether Walker's article was written before or after Karen Sinclair's. Neither scholar cites the other, but both approach Le Guin's work from an anthropological perspective. Walker seems more conversant with modern anthropology than Sinclair, but both take as a starting point the theories of Claude Lévi-Strauss. Lévi-Strauss sees myth as a valuable means of understanding the way a culture thinks. Myth mediates the oppositions at the heart of any culture. Myth is also related to all forms of social exchange in that it records the basic rules of that exchange for a given society. According to Walker, examining the myths Le Guin has created for the Gethenians is an excellent way to approach *The Left Hand of Darkness*.

Walker divides the novel's chapters into two types — mythic and historical — and claims that the mythic chapters act as models for the historical events. Kinship exchange is the most important theme in the myths. In effect, the Gethenian myths explain the rules of kinship in society — the kinds of social exchange that are permitted and the kinds that are forbidden. In order for the family group to grow in strength and influence, members must make alliances outside the family; thus there is a taboo on long-term incest. The Gethenian myths deal with some of the prohibitions in that society and prove that "denials of the law of exchange result in the death of either the individual or the community because both individuals and communities require exchange, not merely for psychological health, but for continued existence" (184). All these myths present patterns of exchange which are followed in the historical sections of the text because the communal myths serve as rules of behavior for the characters who are members of that community.

Walker's analyses are always thought-provoking. She does close readings of Le Guin's works, and her anthropological background allows her to connect with Le Guin's similar background. Le Guin's works are always underpinned by her own knowledge of anthropology, gleaned from her reading and a childhood spent among professional anthropologists.

In an article in the September 1980 issue of the British science fiction journal *Foundation*, Kathleen Spencer once again brings up the subject of the anthropologist hero. Many of her observations repeat those of earlier critics, but she adds to the mix the ideas of Victor Turner on liminality. Although Le Guin's main characters are isolated, they are isolated without being alienated; this is what Turner means by liminality. Because they are liminal, these characters are able to act "out of a profound sense of their own beings" (34). The liminal character can facilitate change in an otherwise conservative community because he or she stands on the border of the community rather than in the middle of it. Liminal status may incorporate complete outsiders as well as low caste members of the community — anyone on the periphery.

According to Spencer, these liminal characters are vital in Le Guin's work:

> Through all her variations of plot and character, this one constant emerges: liminality is the essential precondition for communication between self and other. When characters fail, wholly or in part, to achieve that kind of communication, they fail because the liminal quality is absent or insufficient or one-sided. When characters succeed, they succeed because, whatever their differences, they come to share the liminal condition enough to reach out and touch the alien other. (37)

Spencer examines liminal characters in "Nine Lives," a story about clones; *The Left Hand of Darkness*, and *The Eye of the Heron*, a generally ignored novel published in 1978. In the short story, the ten identical clones are so complete in their oneness that they are almost unaware of others. When an accident leaves only one clone alive, he must learn to be aware of the alien other. In *Left Hand* Genly Ai and Estraven are both liminal characters. In *The Eye of the Heron*, the liminality of a female character, Luz, enables her to leave her own constricting society (where all women are liminal) and lead a group of people from a more open community to a new place of freedom. Luz is the only one capable of seeing the possibilities for the future, because she alone is liminal in both communities.

It is surprising that critics don't take more note of *The Eye of the Heron*, since it marks a feminist epiphany for Le Guin. Before 1978 her science fiction works (with the exception of a few stories) were written from the perspective of male characters, as feminist critics were constantly pointing out. Despite her self-identification as a feminist, Le Guin did not choose to write from a woman's perspective. As she confesses in the essay "The Fisherwoman's Daughter," she didn't know how to write about women. Only in one novel, the Earthsea fantasy *The Tombs of Atuan*, had she successfully sustained the perspective of a female character. Her most successful female main character in science fiction was the old woman Odo in the short story "The Day Before the Revolution." Le Guin desired a way to resolve her own conflict about how to write like a woman, but she had not figured out a solution. She had intended to have a balanced male and female perspective in *The Dispossessed*, but the man Shevek took over the story. Halfway into writing *The Eye of the Heron*, however, her peace-loving male protagonist, Lev, suddenly (and without her conscious intention) got himself shot dead, and his creator was stymied. She set the story aside to give herself time to think. When she returned to it, she discovered that the real protagonist of the story was Luz Marina, a girl trapped in a macho culture, who had originally been a secondary character — a love interest for Lev. As finally published, the story contains several perspectives, both male and female, but it is in the end Luz's story. Le Guin had broken through her difficulties, and from this time on she had no trouble writing science fiction (or any other kind of fiction) with female protagonists.

The Eye of the Heron originally appeared in 1978 as a novella in *Millennial Women*, edited by Virginia Kidd (Le Guin's agent), but it was published as a separate novel that same year. Many of Le Guin's novels followed a similar publication route: novella or short story in a collection or magazine, then separate publication as a book. Thus, "The Tombs of Atuan" in the magazine *Worlds of Fantasy* immediately became Atheneum's *The Tombs of Atuan*; "The Lathe of Heaven" appeared in two parts in *Amazing* magazine the same year Scribner's published the novel version; four years after Ellison's anthology *Again, Dangerous Visions*, "The Word for World Is Forest" became a book. Le Guin critics do not always know whether they are discussing a short story or a book when they talk about these titles; they are generally unaware of the publication history.

Le Guin was a prolific author in the early years of her writing career, but her production slowed in the 1980s, thus allowing scholars an opportunity to catch up. The 1980s saw a continuation of articles and essay collections about Le Guin, but they also witnessed a new spurt of doctoral dissertations and monographs (sometimes based on the dissertations). In the 1970s, four Ph.D. theses were based partly or entirely on Le Guin's work; in the 1980s, sixteen Ph.D. candidates focused on Le Guin, and two of them went on to publish books about her. Le Guin notes that most of these theses were written by women.

Scholars with knowledge from fields outside science fiction and children's literature began to show more of an interest in Le Guin in the 1980s. Linguists, medievalists, philosophers, ecologists, futurists, and others discovered that Le Guin's work offered riches untold. Even though many of them tended to spin her gold into straw, the new approaches to her work inevitably produced new insights. One of the intriguing new investigations appeared in *Mosaic* in 1981. "The Visionary Voyage in Science Fiction and Medieval Allegory," by Laurel Braswell, was a comparative study of two different modes of writing, which, according to Braswell, were remarkably similar. Once again, Le Guin was chosen as one of the representatives of science fiction for comparative purposes (the other two were Roger Zelazny and Samuel Delany).

Braswell compares an early type of Christian writing — the visionary voyage — to modern science fiction. (Considering Le Guin's views on allegory and on Christianity, this is not an approach that she would appreciate, since it tends to read her fiction allegorically and through a Christian lens.) Braswell explains that medieval allegory came in three forms: the debate, the dream vision, and the journey. The final type is the connecting point between allegory and science fiction. Most science fiction is presented as a journey. Both types of literature also provide a means for judging the so-called "real world." As Braswell says, "The measuring, whether explicit or implicit, of the real world against the visionary appears to be one of the basic links between medieval allegory and science fiction" (128). In science fiction, the journey often involves a mission that can easily be interpreted in Christian terms; for example, in *The Left Hand of Darkness* it would be easy to see Genly Ai as the representative of the "redeemed" members of the Ekumen sent to "save" the "fallen" planet of Gethen.

Braswell also sees technical similarities between the two types of literature. Both employ "qualitative names, that is, names which give linguistic indications of some abstract meaning" (133). Genly Ai's name, for instance, contains as much significance as that of Everyman; Le Guin says his last name is a cry of pain in many languages. Another similarity is that just as medieval allegory uses iconographic landscapes, science fiction also provides symbolic landscapes. Gethen's name translates to "Winter," and the frozen landscape Le Guin creates signifies much more than simply a cold climate. Like allegory, science fiction also contains authoritative guides; in *Left Hand* Estraven serves as such a guide for Genly Ai. Finally, the use of Biblical and Classical mythology in medieval allegory is paralleled by the myths Le Guin creates for Gethen. Braswell even claims that

Chaucer would interpret *The Left Hand of Darkness* as an allegory. (I must say that the image of Chaucer reading *The Left Hand of Darkness* is one that boggles the mind.)

An article in the July 1981 issue of *Science-Fiction Studies* returns to the idea of dualism. In "Le Guin's Twofold Vision: Contrary Image-Sets in *The Left Hand of Darkness*," David J. Lake expands the dualistic images beyond those of dark and light. He claims there are two basic sets of images, which he terms the "warm" team and the "cold" team. The words he associates with the cold team are cold, light, white, ice, pale liquids, and left. The warm team consists of images based on the words warmth, darkness, red, earth, blood, and right. According to Lake, "the 'cold team' images correlate with each other and symbolize rationalism, certain knowledge, tyranny, isolation, betrayal, death; and the 'warm team' images correlate with each other and symbolize intuition, ignorance, freedom, relationship, fidelity, life" (156). Lake also wants to have the cold team represent the nation of Karhide (Estraven's feudalistic country) and the warm team represent the repressive, communistic country of Orgoreyn.

Lake's thesis is far too dogmatic for a novel as complex as *The Left Hand of Darkness*, but when he examines specific images, he often makes interesting observations. For example, he notes that in the novel red light is never bright, but is rather a kind of visible darkness. He also points out how the Karhide religion, based on darkness, is favored by the author over the Orgoreyn religion that worships only light. Lake sees parallels between this second religion, the Yomesh cult, and Christianity. The Yomesh cult believes in saints and angels, rejects darkness entirely, and uses a dating system based on the death of their savior, Meshe. As Lake suggests, "May we not also suspect that the name 'Meshe' is meant to suggest not only 'mesh of a net' but also 'Messiah'?" (160). Since the values of Orgoreyn emerge from the Yomesh beliefs, Le Guin is criticizing the historical results of Christianity's influence on the West.

The first book-length monograph on Le Guin also appeared in 1981. It shared the same title as most books about the author: simply *Ursula K. Le Guin*. This one was a volume in the Frederick Unger series Recognitions, which focuses on individual authors of fiction in the so-called popular genres (mainly science fiction and detective fiction). The author, Barbara J. Bucknall, presents a general overview of Le Guin's work but is primarily interested in the fantasy and science fiction. The book seems to be aimed at a general audience, so there is little in-depth criticism; there are long plot summaries supplemented with obvious commentary. However, Bucknall does make several intriguing observations in passing. For example, she points out that *The Left Hand of Darkness* is basically the same story as *The Tombs of Atuan* but is told with more complexity. This is an unusual connection to make, but Bucknall sees Estraven relating to Genly the same way Tenar relates to Ged in *Tombs*: the female or seemingly female member of each pair rescues the male, but there is no happy ever after. Both novels are concerned with fidelity and betrayal.

In discussing *The Lathe of Heaven*, Bucknall notices (and is apparently the first commentator to do so) that Dr. Haber exists only because George Orr has dreamed him up in an effective dream that occurred before the novel opens. In dreaming away an atomic explosion, Orr has dreamed up a psychiatrist to help him stop dreaming. This is a rich area for further exploration, but the nature of Bucknall's volume does not allow her to continue into such detailed criticism. Bucknall also points out that Orr's character is a tribute to Philip K. Dick, a science fiction writer admired by Le Guin, who specializes in ordinary characters with extraordinary abilities.

In 1982 the journal *Names* published "Magic Names: Onomastics in the Fantasies of Ursula Le Guin," an article by John Algeo that examines Le Guin's use of proper names. As the title indicates, Algeo is mostly interested in the proper names used in the Earthsea books. But he also discusses names in *The Lathe of Heaven*. Algeo claims that Le Guin's naming techniques in her science fiction are different from those in her fantasy. The names in Earthsea are chosen for their sound, whereas the science fiction names are open to more intellectual analysis, he claims.

George Orr, the main character in *The Lathe of Heaven*, is a tribute to George Orwell, as many critics have noted. According to Algeo, though, there is much more meaning in his name. The name George means "farmer," and George Orr is a person who causes things to grow — his effective dreams grow into reality. Algeo sees the last name Orr as a double pun on "or" and "ore." The first pun is obvious in the novel, in which one character refers to George as "Mr. Either Orr." George measures in the exact middle of every psychological test he takes, and he appears to be indecisive about everything. George's mind is also the raw ore from which new worlds are created. Algeo points out a specific link to Orwell that has been overlooked by other critics: in the novel the United States has undergone a complete revolution resulting in a police state, and the revolution occurred in 1984.

Algeo also sees significance in the name of George's abusive psychiatrist, William Haber. His first name is an acrostic for "I am will," indicating the power of his self-will, which is his dominant characteristic. His last name is similar to a German word for "have" or "possess," and certainly possession and control are Haber's goals in his attempts to force George to dream according to the doctor's directions.

Just in case anyone is tempted to think Algeo is overreaching in his interpretation of these names, he quotes from Le Guin's introduction to her short story "The Ones who Walk Away from Omelas." She found the name Omelas from reading a road sign backwards: Salem, Oregon. In the introduction in *The Wind's Twelve Quarters*, Le Guin lists the connotations Omelas has for her: "Salem equals schelomo equals salaam equals Peace. Melas. O melas. Omelas. Homme hélas" (*Wind's Twelve Quarters* 225). As Algeo properly concludes, anyone who can make such elaborate onomastic connections in her own mind is capable of creating proper names with unlimited connotations.

Philosophy entered the critical mix in 1982 in a collection of essays called *Philosophers Look at Science Fiction*. This volume resulted from the 1978 conference of the Science Fiction Research Association, at which meeting Le Guin was a special guest. Although several of the articles mention Le Guin, only one is noteworthy here, Wayne Cogell's "The Absurdity of Sartre's Ontology: A Response by Ursula K. Le Guin." Cogell examines a little known Le Guin story, "A Trip to the Head," which was included in *The Wind's Twelve Quarters* (1975).

Cogell, a professor of philosophy, claims that "A Trip to the Head" is a *reductio ad absurdum* of Sartre's existential philosophy. Cogell's thesis clarifies this claim:

> Le Guin calls attention to three absurdities in Sartre's philosophy: first, the arbitrariness and lack of firm grounds in Sartre's account of human choice, which makes ethics meaningless; second, the exclusive emphasis on subjective time, which results in solipsism; and third, the emphasis on self-created essence, which makes significant interpersonal human relations impossible. (144)

In Sartre's philosophy, the appearance of things is their reality; humans must define their own meaning and create their own essence, which may be modified by the actions of others. Everyone has a great potential for nothingness. In Le Guin's story, two characters who don't even know their own names go through a series of nonsensical, arbitrary, and meaningless actions. According to Cogell, Le Guin is attempting to show what a world constructed according to Sartre's philosophy would be like. Since Le Guin lives by a strong set of moral principles, a philosophy that discounts ethics is bound to be anathema to her. For Le Guin, Sartre's concepts are absurd. That "A Trip to the Head" is clearly a commentary on Sartre is obvious from the many references to Sartre in the story.

Because of the nature of Sartrean philosophy, both the philosophy and the short story are difficult to explicate. Cogell's article is therefore not a model of clarity; however, it is an interesting attempt to bring philosophical discourse into Le Guin criticism. Linguists seem to have an easier time of it: their terms are not as abstract as those of philosophy, and application of their concepts is more direct. Of course, the linguists also tend to choose more comprehensible texts as well. Closely related to linguistics is the study of communication, which also appears in Le Guin criticism.

Virginia Myers takes a communication approach to *The Left Hand of Darkness* in a 1983 article, "Conversational Technique in Ursula Le Guin: A Speech-Act Analysis." She points out the linguistic difficulty faced by a science fiction writer who wants to create aliens who are believably different from us and yet also wants to provide a means of understanding those aliens. There must be barriers to communication, including linguistic ones, but there must also be a way to get over or through those barriers. Because Le Guin sets up the Gethenian languages to operate according to the same principles as languages on Earth, it is possible to approach communication in *Left Hand* by means of speech-act theory.

Since Myers is writing for the *Science-Fiction Studies* audience, she first spends some time explaining speech-act theory. Without repeating her careful explanation, much of her argument is lost, but in general terms, speech-act theory tries to explain how communication works by looking at the intentions, cultural assumptions, and mental and emotional condition of both speaker and hearer. Examining the conversations of characters on the basis of speech-act theory, Myers shows that Genly Ai is fooling himself when he claims to misunderstand Estraven's advice because of its indirectness; as a hearer, Genly refuses to cooperate in interpreting Estraven's speech act because he misunderstands the other's motives. On other occasions, Genly has no difficulty understanding the indirect speech acts of the Gethenians. He willfully chooses to misinterpret Estraven's words.

According to Myers, Le Guin uses different types of speech acts to show the developing relationship between Genly and Estraven. The author also shows each character developing more consciousness of the meaning of the speech acts. As Myers points out, "Confessions of fault, avowals of belief, apologies — expressed in direct form — appear in greater proportion after Estraven rescues Genly Ai from near death in Pulefen Voluntary Farm" (311). These kinds of speech acts make the characters more vulnerable to each other and allow understanding to grow. Their earlier speech acts had been mostly questions and assertions; a change in the type of speech act reflects the changing relationship.

Estraven eventually learns to transcend the linguistic customs of his culture so that he can use direct speech acts with Genly, who clearly values the direct variety over the Gethenians' standard indirect speech act. On the other hand, Genly learns to correctly interpret Estraven's intentions and no longer needs the same level of directness. All of this, says Myers, shows that Le Guin has a complex understanding of how communication works in personal relationships.

In summer of 1984 *Modern Language Studies* published an interesting article about Le Guin's treatment of old age. "'Only in dying, life': the Dynamics of Old Age in the Fiction of Ursula Le Guin" was written by Charlotte Spivack, who was at that time completing a volume on Le Guin for Twayne's United States Authors series. In this article Spivack looks at Le Guin's presentation of three older characters: Wold, the patriarch of a tribal society in *Planet of Exile*; Odo, the female anarchist of "The Day Before the Revolution"; and the mature Ged of *The Farthest Shore*. Le Guin presents these characters as dynamic and ambivalent individuals rather than as stereotypes.

Although Wold is a minor character, Spivack sees him as a fully rounded one. In *Planet of Exile*, Wold is the nominal leader of his people, but he has little authority left. However, in Le Guin's portrayal, Wold remains internally vibrant while limited by physical weakness, and his brave decision to join the alien colonizers in fighting off an invasion from another tribe leads to a glorious future for his people, even though it causes his own death.

"The Day Before the Revolution" is a kind of prologue to *The Dispossessed*. It concerns the last day of Odo's life. Her strength and spirit have created a new way of thinking that will lead to the establishment of an anarchic society on her planet's moon, but at the time of the story she is an old woman facing her own death and her own accomplishments with ambivalence. According to Spivack, the graphic details of Odo's last day build a convincing portrait of dynamic old age. None of these elderly characters is weak or useless, and all are individuals who can still affect their societies.

The Twayne volume on Le Guin also came out in 1984; the *Modern Language Studies* article was clearly an offshoot of that larger project. Spivack's monograph is called, naturally, *Ursula K. Le Guin*. Like Barbara Bucknall's book of the same title, this work is intended for general readers. But it is more scholarly than the Bucknall volume. Spivack lists Le Guin's main themes as cultural anthropology, Jungian psychology, and Taoism. Other critics have discussed the hero as anthropologist, but Spivack points out that the anthropological outlook requires a person to be coolly sympathetic but detached. (Le Guin exhibits the same qualities as a narrator.)

Spivack notes that Le Guin's early science fiction, although not as important as her later works, is more fun to read. This early work contains the same plot structure Le Guin uses in all her novels: "In this plot structure an isolated and alienated hero journeys to a strange far-away place where, through a series of contacts with creatures alien to him, he discovers himself" (9). Le Guin seldom uses villains in her work, says Spivack, because she does not view things as good or evil. She takes a position of moral relativity — any action can be either good or bad.

Spivack's book is the best of the monographs on Le Guin. Her analysis of the novels is detailed and persuasive, and she attempts to discuss the variety of Le Guin's work. Spivack's own strength is in science fiction, however; her discussion of Le Guin's poetry is mechanical, and she knows very little about the field of children's literature. As an introduction to the work of Le Guin, the Twayne volume is excellent, but the best of the in-depth criticism is found in journal articles.

Yet another monograph on Le Guin was published in 1984 — James W. Bittner's *Approaches to the Fiction of Ursula K. Le Guin*. For once the title was distinguishable from the previous author studies. This book was Bittner's dissertation, published by Ann Arbor's UMI Research Press as the fourth volume in the series Studies in Speculative Fiction. The series editor was Robert Scholes, who had already proven his interest in Le Guin.

Bittner is interested in proving that all of Le Guin's works are romances. He approaches his discussion through the ideas of Kathryn Hume (herself building on Joseph Campbell), who sees three stages in the development of the romance hero's ego development: equilibrium, struggle, and higher harmony. This is the pattern Bittner seeks in all of Le Guin's novels, including the fantasy, the science fiction, and the historical. He says "the plot of nearly every piece of fiction Le Guin writes is the distinctively Romantic spiral journey back home" (58).

Bittner points out how much Norse myth has influenced Le Guin. For example, "The Dowry of Angyar," the short story that became the prequel for *Rocannon's World*, is simply a retelling of the Norse myth of Freya's necklace. Rocannon himself becomes a reincarnation of Odin. Bittner also finds Teutonic and Celtic myth in the Earthsea fantasies. Other critics have also traced particular mythologies through Le Guin's works, but Bittner's discussion is more sustained than most.

Bittner is also interested in showing how all of Le Guin's books work together. She wrote her science fiction novels and fantasy novels in paired sets: *A Wizard of Earthsea* and *The Left Hand of Darkness* are one pair; *The Tombs of Atuan* and *The Lathe of Heaven* form a second; and *The Farthest Shore* and *The Dispossessed* make up a third. According to Bittner, these are complementary works. At the same time she was writing these books, Le Guin was also working on books about her imaginary historical country of Orsinia, so that side of her creativity is also involved in the fantasy and science fiction. Rather than Earthsea, the Hainish universe, and

Orsinia being three strands of creativity, they are in reality parts of one another.

When he discusses the early science fiction, Bittner finds a connection that has been missed by other critics. Le Guin calls her reconstructed League of All Worlds the Ekumen, which has led some scholars to find a link to Christianity, but Bittner shows how Le Guin could instead have garnered the term from her anthropologist father, Alfred Kroeber (as indeed she did, the author confirms). In his own theory of culture, Kroeber adapted the Greek word Oikoumene to refer to a common origin for the ecumenical Eurasian cultures. Le Guin could have borrowed the word from her father, as well as the notion that all the inhabited planets had a common origin from being seeded by the ancient Hainish. Bittner's explanation is in any case more persuasive than those of critics who connect the Ekumen with Christianity.

Another suggestion Bittner makes is that Le Guin's experiments with point of view are due to her realization that authorial omniscience is a kind of imperialism. The League of All Worlds is exploitative and imperialistic, but its successor, the Ekumen, has evolved into a loose cultural cooperative. In the same way, the structure of Le Guin's narrative changes to reflect a more cooperative and egalitarian way of storytelling. This explains the unusual structure of *The Left Hand of Darkness*. If these changes are due to Le Guin's own thought processes, then she independently came to the same conclusions as some feminist theorists about the effects a patriarchal culture has on political and literary structures.

In 1986 another strong feminist criticism of *Left Hand* was published in the essay collection *Erotic Universe: Sexuality and Fantastic Literature*. In their article "Again, *The Left Hand of Darkness*: Androgyny or Homophobia?" Patricia Frazer Lamb and Diana L. Veith examine whether Le Guin's presentation of androgyny shows signs of homophobia. Because both Genly Ai and Estraven are presented as socially and psychologically masculine, the love that develops between them must be perceived as homosexual. Le Guin does not permit these two characters to explore their love physically, and Estraven virtually commits suicide at the end of the story by skiing directly toward armed guards who have orders to shoot him on sight. As Lamb and Veith conclude, "The unmistakable message is that death is the price that must be paid for forbidden love" (228). Le Guin was aware that she had presented heterosexuality as the norm on Gethen, and she apologized for this result of her cultural conditioning in the 1989 article "Is Gender Necessary? Redux."

Lamb and Veith view Estraven as a romantic hero in the Byronic tradition; therefore, the kind of love most attractive to him would be a forbidden kind, such as the vow of sexual fidelity to his own brother, which resulted in the brother's suicide and Estraven's exile. Romantic love is always forbidden or dangerous in some way. The events of the novel and the way Le Guin portrays them clearly show that *Left Hand* is firmly within the romantic tradition, as other critics have suggested.

1986 was the year the prolific critic Harold Bloom incorporated Le Guin into his vast publishing machine. Bloom got considerable mileage out of Le Guin: he published two collections of essays back-to-back. In 1986 he put together a volume on Le Guin for Chelsea House, which once again adopted the default title, *Ursula K. Le Guin*. Bloom republished many of the articles I have already discussed, and he attached an introduction that generally repeats the findings of previous critics. What Bloom adds to the criticism is the observation that Le Guin's works contain quite a bit of sly humor, that she is a much better writer than a critic, and that Genly Ai plays Horatio to Estraven's Hamlet. In 1987 Bloom produced a second collection of essays on Le Guin for Chelsea House, *Ursula K. Le Guin's The Left Hand of Darkness*. This time the volume concentrated on *The Left Hand of Darkness* as Le Guin's masterpiece. This second volume not only reproduces the same introduction as the first book, but it also includes six of the articles from the 1986 collection. Bloom gets incredible publication mileage out of other people's work. He also manages to copyright the exact same introduction twice. What he doesn't do is contribute anything substantial to Le Guin criticism. Considering his critical reputation and the number of original publications to his credit, I don't understand why he would bother with this kind of recycling job. Perhaps he simply wished to throw his critical weight behind Le Guin to bring her work to the attention of readers outside of science fiction.

One of the standard approaches to Le Guin criticism is to compare her to another writer. *Foundation, Extrapolation,* and *Science-Fiction Studies* all have published articles that compare Le Guin to other science fiction writers. Generally such articles add little critical insight to the understanding of Le Guin's contribution to literature. Every now and then, however, a comparative study can reveal previously unnoticed aspects of Le Guin's work.

One such article is Richard D. Erlich's "Ursula K. Le Guin and Arthur C. Clarke on Immanence, Transcendence, and Massacres," which appeared in the summer 1987 issue of *Extrapolation*. Erlich has chosen a good basis of comparison for these two authors. As he shows in the article, although they share many interests and images, their basic approach to existence is quite different. In their attitude toward reality, Clarke favors transcendence while Le Guin favors immanence. Characters in Clarke's work transcend their human limits and find change in an outward expansion. Le Guin's characters must look within for change. These are two different aspects of the spiritual.

In the following year Robert Scholes shepherded a second dissertation on Le Guin through the process of publication for UMI Research Press's Studies in Speculative Fiction. Number 16 of that series was published in 1988 as *Le Guin and Identity in Contemporary Fiction*, by Bernard Selinger. Selinger is concerned with the formation of identity in Freudian terms. Both Le Guin and her characters have a problem with blurred boundaries, he claims, resulting in loss of ego. He combs all the novels for Freudian symbols, such as phallic staffs, and equates certain passages with Freud's developmental stages, as in this comment about the journey over the deadly ice in *The Left Hand of Darkness*: "The journey charts the precarious course the infant takes in its early months, when it is still dependent on the symbiotic unit yet is just barely beginning to realize some need for differentiation" (61). Selinger identifies several of Le Guin's characters as autistic children — for instance, George Orr in *The Lathe of Heaven* is autistic because he is associated with eggs and an egg was Freud's symbol for autism. As an exercise in applied theory, Selinger's book is interesting, but it does not shed any real light on Le Guin. Although most of the reading is Freudian, Selinger also drags in Lacan, Bruno Bettelheim, Julia Kristeva, Eric Erikson, Jacques Derrida, and others, so the theories get tangled up in a confusing heap before the end of the book. This is not one of the high points of Le Guin criticism.

The fall 1989 issue of *Extrapolation* contains another comparative essay. "Adult Telepathy: *Babel-17* and *The Left Hand of Darkness*," by Susan Stone-Blackburn, compares *Left Hand* to a science fiction novel by Samuel Delany. After a brief overview of how telepathy has been presented in science fiction — generally as a mutation that creates a superbeing — Stone-Blackburn says both Le Guin and Delany have a different view of telepathy in which it is "at least in part a learned, intellectual attainment, an outgrowth of linguistic sophistication, consciously cultivated and voluntarily employed" (246). In both of the novels under discussion, a telepathic union between two main characters is presented as the emotional climax of the story. However, the two authors have approached the idea of such a union from different directions: "Delany arrives at telepathy by probing the relationship between language and thought; Le Guin, by absorbing the Tao, with its emphasis on the underlying unity of all things" (249). Both authors employ a telepathic union rather than a sexual one.

Another 1989 article in *Extrapolation* shows how three characters in "The Word for World Is Forest" exemplify different aspects of American attitudes toward the environment. In "Visions of Nature in *The Word for World is Forest*: A Mirror of the American Consciousness," Carol P. Hovanec discusses Davidson, Lyubov, and Selver as representatives of three historical attitudes toward nature. Captain Davidson, the macho imperialist, exemplifies the attitude of early explorers and settlers who wished to conquer the environment and who feared the wilderness. Davidson even thinks about the conquistadors and sees himself in a similar role. Lyubov, the anthropologist, has ambivalent feelings about the wilderness. On the whole, though, he exhibits the attitude of the romantics toward nature, idealizing it and seeing the native inhabitants as noble savages. The natives themselves exemplify a more modern attitude toward nature — the desire and ability to live in perfect harmony with their surroundings. In effect, this story tells the complete history of American attitudes toward nature. My own biases in favor of historical and cultural criticism may be influencing my judgment in including Hovanec's article as a critical highlight; many of her observations are obvious to a reader with any knowledge of American history. But her article would certainly be insightful and informative for a reader who lacks a historical background.

Yet another introductory overview of Le Guin's works came out in 1990. Elizabeth Cummins (the same Elizabeth Cummins Cogell who compiled the excellent bibliography on Le Guin) contributed a volume called *Understanding Ursula K. Le Guin* to a series published by the University of South Carolina Press. Although not as valuable as the bibliography, this volume does contribute to Le Guin criticism. Cummins sees Le Guin's main interests as world building and storytelling. The author has created four alternate realities: the Hainish universe, Earthsea, Orsinia, and the future West Coast. Cummins discusses the four separate realities in different chapters. As an introduction to Le Guin's works, this is a fine volume for undergraduate students and lay readers, which is the purpose of the series, but it does not contain any in-depth commentary. Cummins does mention many of the important insights into Le Guin which other critics have contributed.

One final article from *Extrapolation* completes this chapter. In 1992 the science fiction journal published Nora Barry and Mary Prescott's "Beyond Words: The Impact of Rhythm as Narrative Technique in *The Left Hand of Darkness.*" Barry and Prescott say that Le Guin is interested in exploring the aspects of reality that cannot be described in conventional ways. One of the unconventional methods she adopts to describe such a reality is rhythm. As the writers explain the term, "Simply defined, rhythm is repetition with enough variation to preclude a hardening into symbolism. Its purpose is expansion, not completion, for it resounds with meaning that is liberated from the mechanics of language and conventional thinking" (156).

Le Guin's method in *Left Hand* is described as "contrapuntal." According to Barry and Prescott, the chapters move back and forth between fact and personal response. This method forces the reader to adapt Genly Ai's outlook as his or her own. Once Le Guin has established certain attitudes toward gender in the reader's mind as well as Genly Ai's, she sets a trap with the chapter "A Question of Sex." This factual explanation of Gethenian sexuality concludes with a reference to the gender of the report writer, who is female. As Barry and Prescott point out, "Because this revelation is irrelevant to the intended readers of the report, leaders of the Ekumen and the First Mobile, it is surprising that any reference to the writer's gender appears at all" (157). That reference is there for Le Guin's readers, so that they can be confronted with the same gender assumptions as Genly Ai. As Genly Ai deals with his own assumptions, readers deal with theirs. This is an example of how Le Guin uses rhythm to express something that cannot be said in words. She uses the same method to disrupt the reader's assumptions about shadow, challenging the common negative connotations of the word through her contrapuntal use of it.

The Left Hand of Darkness has garnered more scholarly commentary than any of Le Guin's other works, except for *A Wizard of Earthsea* and *The Dispossessed*, which have drawn equal attention. *Left Hand* is at the center of the feminist controversy over Le Guin, just as *Wizard* is the focus of all the fantasy criticism. *The Dispossessed* marks a change in emphasis for both author and critics. Since most of the criticism of *The Dispossessed* concentrates on its utopian aspects, it will be the focal point of the next chapter.

Works Cited

Algeo, John. "Magic Names: Onomastics in the Fantasies of Ursula Le Guin." *Names* 30.2 (1982): 59–67.

Bangsund, John. Rev. of *City of Illusions. Australian Science Fiction Review* 10 (June 1967): 65–66.

Barbour, Douglas. "*The Lathe of Heaven*: Taoist Dream." *Algol* 21 (November 1973): 22–24.

———. "On Ursula Le Guin's *A Wizard of Earthsea*." *Riverside Quarterly* 6 (April 1974): 19–23.

———. "Patterns and Meaning in the Novels of Ursula K. Le Guin, Joanna Russ and Samuel R. Delany, 1962–1972." Ph.D. dissertation, Queen's University (Canada), 1976.

———. "Wholeness and Balance in the Hainish Novels of Ursula K. Le Guin." *Science-Fiction Studies* 1 (Spring 1974): 164–73.

Barry, Nora, and Mary Prescott. "Beyond Words: The Impact of Rhythm as Narrative Technique in *The Left Hand of Darkness.*" *Extrapolation* 33 (Summer 1992): 154–65.

Bickman, Martin. "Le Guin's *The Left Hand of Darkness*: Form and Content." *Science-Fiction Studies* 4 (March 1977). *Ursula K. Le Guin's The Left Hand of Darkness.* Ed. Harold Bloom. Modern Critical Interpretations. New York: Chelsea House, 1987. 53–62.

Bittner, James W. *Approaches to the Fiction of Ursula K. Le Guin.* Studies in Speculative Fiction 4. Ann Arbor: UMI Research Press, 1984.

Bloom, Harold, ed. *Ursula K. Le Guin.* Modern Critical Views. New York: Chelsea House, 1986.

——. *Ursula K. Le Guin's The Left Hand of Darkness.* Modern Critical Interpretations. New York: Chelsea House, 1987.

Braswell, Laurel. "The Visionary Voyage in Science Fiction and Medieval Allegory." *Mosaic* 14 (Winter 1981): 125–42.

Bucknall, Barbara J. *Ursula K. Le Guin.* New York: Frederick Ungar, 1981.

Cawthorn, James. "I Love You, Semantics." Rev. of *Rocannon's World. New Worlds* 49 (August 1966): 147.

Cogell, Wayne. "The Absurdity of Sartre's Ontology: A Response by Ursula K. Le Guin." *Philosophers Look at Science Fiction.* Ed. Nicholas D. Smith. Chicago: Nelson-Hall, 1982. 143–51.

Cummins, Elizabeth. *Understanding Ursula K. Le Guin.* Columbia, SC: U of South Carolina P, 1990.

Davidson, Avram. *The Kar-Chee Reign.* New York: Ace, 1966.

Disch, Thomas M. *Mankind Under the Leash.* New York: Ace, 1966.

Erlich, Richard D. "Ursula K. Le Guin and Arthur C. Clarke on Immanence, Transcendence, and Massacres." *Extrapolation* 28 (Summer 1987): 105–29.

Friend, Beverly. "Virgin Territory: Women and Sex in Science Fiction." *Extrapolation* 14 (December 1972): 49–58.

Gunew, Sneja. "Mythic Reversals: The Evolution of the Shadow Motif." *Ursula K. Le Guin.* Ed. Joseph D. Olander and Martin Harry Greenberg. Writers of the 21st Century Series. New York: Taplinger, 1979. 178–99.

Hayles, N. B. "Androgyny, Ambivalence, and Assimilation in *The Left Hand of Darkness.*" *Ursula K. Le Guin.* Ed. Joseph D. Olander and Martin Harry Greenberg. Writers of the 21st Century Series. New York: Taplinger, 1979. 97–115.

Hovanec, Carol P. "Visions of Nature in *The Word for World is Forest*: A Mirror of the American Consciousness." *Extrapolation* 30 (Spring 1989): 84–91.

Huntington, John. "Public and Private Imperatives in Le Guin's Novels." *Science-Fiction Studies* 2 (November 1975): 237–43.

Ketterer, David. "In Response." *Science-Fiction Studies* 2 (July 1975): 139–46.

———. *New Worlds for Old: The Apocalyptic Imagination, Science Fiction, and American Literature*. Bloomington: Indiana UP, 1974.

Koper, Peter T. "Science and Rhetoric in the Fiction of Ursula Le Guin." *Ursula K. Le Guin: Voyager to Inner Lands and to Outer Space*. Ed. Joe De Bolt. Literary Criticism Series. Port Washington, NY: Kennikat Press, 1979. 66–86.

Lake, David J. "Le Guin's Twofold Vision: Contrary Image-Sets in *The Left Hand of Darkness*." *Science-Fiction Studies* 8 (July 1981): 156–64.

Lamb, Patricia Frazer, and Diana L. Veith. "Again, *The Left Hand of Darkness*: Androgyny or Homophobia?" *Erotic Universe: Sexuality and Fantastic Literature*. Ed. Donald Palumbo. Contributions to the Study of Science Fiction and Fantasy 18. Westport, CT: Greenwood Press, 1986. 221–31.

Le Guin, Ursula K. "April in Paris." *Fantastic* 11 (September 1962): 54–65.

———. *City of Illusions*. New York: Ace, 1967. New York: Garland, 1975.

———. "Darkness Box." *Fantastic* 12 (November 1963): 60–67.

———. "The Day Before the Revolution." *Galaxy* 35 (August 1974): 17–30.

———. *The Dispossessed: An Ambiguous Utopia*. New York: Harper & Row, 1974.

———. "The Dowry of Angyar." *Amazing* 38 (September 1964): 46–63.

———. *The Eye of the Heron*. New York: Harper & Row, 1978.

———. "The Fisherwoman's Daughter." *Dancing at the Edge of the World: Thoughts on Words, Women, Places*. New York: Harper & Row/Perennial Library, 1990. 212–37.

———. "Is Gender Necessary?" *Aurora: Beyond Equality*. Ed. Vonda N. McIntyre and Susan Janice Anderson. Greenwich: Fawcett, 1976. 130–39.

———. "Is Gender Necessary? Redux." *The Language of the Night*. Rev. ed. London: Women's Press, 1989. New York: HarperCollins, 1992. 155–72.

———. "Ketterer on *The Left Hand of Darkness*." *Science-Fiction Studies* 2 (July 1975): 137–39.

———. *The Language of the Night*. Ed. Susan Wood. G. P. Putnam's, 1979. New York: Berkley, 1985.

———. *The Language of the Night*. Revised ed. London: Women's Press, 1989. New York: HarperCollins, 1992.

———. *The Lathe of Heaven*. New York: Scribner's, 1971.

———. *The Left Hand of Darkness*. New York: Ace, 1969.

———. Letter to the editor. *SF Commentary* 26 (April 1971): 90–93.

———. "The Masters." *Fantastic* 12 (February 1963): 85–99.

——. "Nine Lives." *Playboy* 16 (November 1969): 128–29, 132, 220–30.

—— "The Ones Who Walk Away from Omelas." *New Dimensions III*. Ed. Robert Silverberg. New York: Signet, 1973.

——. *Planet of Exile*. New York: Ace, 1966. New York: Garland, 1975.

——. *Rocannon's World*. New York: Ace, 1966. New York: Garland, 1975.

——. "Selection." *Amazing* 38 (August 1964): 36–45.

——. *The Tombs of Atuan*. New York: Atheneum, 1971.

——. "A Trip to the Head." *The Wind's Twelve Quarters*. New York: Harper & Row, 1975. 142–47.

——. "Vaster Than Empires and More Slow." *New Dimensions I*. Ed. Robert Silverberg. Garden City: Doubleday, 1971. 87–121.

——. *The Wind's Twelve Quarters*. New York: Harper & Row, 1975.

——. *A Wizard of Earthsea*. Berkeley: Parnassus Press, 1968.

——. "The Word for World Is Forest." *Again, Dangerous Visions*. Ed. Harlan Ellison. Garden City: Doubleday, 1972. 30–108.

Lem, Stanislaw. "Lost Opportunities." *SF Commentary* 24 (November 1971): 22–24.

Merril, Judith. Rev. of *Rocannon's World*. *Fantasy and Science Fiction* 31 (December 1966): 33.

Miller, P. Schuyler. Rev. of *Rocannon's World*. *Analog* 80 (November 1967): 166.

Myers, Victoria. "Conversational Techniques in Ursula Le Guin: A Speech-Act Analysis." *Science-Fiction Studies* 10 (November 1983): 306–16.

"Myths of Anti-Climax." Rev. of *The Lathe of Heaven*. *Times Literary Supplement* 23 June 1972: 705.

Nudelman, Rafail. "An Approach to the Structure of Le Guin's SF." *Science-Fiction Studies* 2 (November 1975): 210–20.

Panshin, Alexei. "Books." Rev. of *The Left Hand of Darkness*. *Fantasy and Science Fiction* 37 (November 1969): 50–51.

Porter, David L. "The Politics of Le Guin's Opus." *Science-Fiction Studies* 2 (November 1975): 243–48.

Remington, Thomas J. "The Other Side of Suffering: Touch as Theme and Metaphor in Le Guin's Science Fiction Novels." *Ursula K. Le Guin*. Ed. Joseph D. Olander and Martin Harry Greenberg. Writers of the 21st Century Series. New York: Taplinger, 1979. 153–77.

Russ, Joanna. "The Image of Women in Science Fiction." *Images of Women in Fiction: Feminist Perspectives*. Ed. Susan Koppelman Cornillon. Bowling Green: Bowling Green U Popular P, 1972. 79–94.

Scholes, Robert. "The Good Witch of the West." *Hollins Critic* 11 (April 1974): 1–12.

——. *Structural Fabulation: An Essay on Fiction of the Future.* Notre Dame: U of Notre Dame P, 1975.

Selinger, Bernard. *Le Guin and Identity in Contemporary Fiction.* Studies in Speculative Fiction 16. Ann Arbor: UMI Research Press, 1988.

Sinclair, Karen. "Solitary Being: The Hero as Anthropologist." *Ursula K. Le Guin: Voyager to Inner Lands and to Outer Space.* Ed. Joe De Bolt. Literary Criticism Series. Port Washington, NY: Kennikat Press, 1979. 50–65.

Slusser, George Edgar. *The Farthest Shores of Ursula K. Le Guin.* Popular Writers of Today 3. San Bernardino: The Borgo Press, 1976.

Spencer, Kathleen. "Exiles and Envoys: The SF of Ursula K. Le Guin." *Foundation* 20 (October 1980): 32–43.

Spivack, Charlotte. "'Only in dying life': the Dynamics of Old Age in the Fiction of Ursula Le Guin." *Modern Language Studies* 14 (Summer 1984): 43–53.

——. *Ursula K. Le Guin.* Twayne's United States Authors Series 453. Boston: Twayne, 1984.

Stone-Blackburn, Susan. "Adult Telepathy: *Babel-17* and *The Left Hand of Darkness.*" *Extrapolation* 30 (Fall 1989): 243–53.

Sturgeon, Theodore. Rev. of *The Lathe of Heaven. New York Times Book Review* 14 May 1972: 33.

Suvin, Darko. "Introductory Note: The Science Fiction of Ursula K. Le Guin." *Science-Fiction Studies* 2 (November 1975): 203–4.

——. "The SF Novel in 1969." *Nebula Award Stories 5.* Ed. James Blish. London: Gollancz, 1970. 193–205.

Walker, Jeanne Murray. "Myth, Exchange and History in *The Left Hand of Darkness. Science-Fiction Studies* 6 (July 1979): 180–89.

Watson, Ian. "The Forest as Metaphor for Mind: 'The Word for World Is Forest' and 'Vaster Than Empires and More Slow.'" *Science-Fiction Studies* 2 (November 1975): 231–37.

3: The Great Good Place

SOMEWHERE OVER THE RAINBOW OR beyond the blue event horizon lies the Great Good Place — Shangri-La, Never Land, the Isles of the Blessed, Paradise, the place Thomas More christened Utopia. In modern usage, a utopia is a vision built on an optimistic desire to create the perfect society or to point out glaring discrepancies in our own. The word itself is a pun in Greek: it can mean "good place" (*eu-topos*) or "no place" (*ou-topos*). Most scholars agree that More meant the latter when he coined the term, but readers who perceive the book to be a satire (which is hard for most of us to judge in the original Latin version of 1516) prefer the pun. More's *Utopia* presents a humanistic and rational alternative to the European society of his day. The book set the standard for all future utopian works, although it was certainly not the first of its kind. Fiction and philosophical treatises that envision the Great Good Place have been around for centuries, going back at least as far as Plato's *Republic*, and they have developed into their own literary genre and field of study, known as Utopian Studies. Utopian Studies incorporates scholars from diverse fields, such as political science, sociology, literature, linguistics, psychology, economics, history, ecology, anthropology, and futurology.

Utopian literature is divided into loosely chronological types. First, there are the classical utopias, philosophical dialogues modeled after Plato's *Republic*, dating back to the fifth century BC. Later there developed a kind of utopian writing now often called the traditional utopia, in which a curious traveler visits a distant utopian place, is given a tour of the new society's wonders, then returns home a changed man (or woman). This is the kind of utopia we hear the most about — More's own eponymous society, Samuel Butler's *Erewhon* (1872), Edward Bellamy's *Looking Backward* (1887). Traditional utopias are static and descriptive, sometimes prescriptive. In the nineteenth century, they were often technological. There was a strong optimism that science and technology would eventually cure society's ills, as well as an idealistic hope that socialism as propounded by people like Karl Marx could tackle social inequities.

After World War I, however, people were less optimistic about science and socialism; optimism decreased further when the great socialist experiment of revolutionary Russia didn't turn out as well as expected and when science enabled us to drop atomic bombs on Japan but not to cure cancer. As a result of lowered optimism about utopian possibilities, a reactionary

form of the genre appeared, called dystopian literature. If a utopia is
heaven on earth, a dystopia is hell on earth. The most famous examples
are Aldous Huxley's *Brave New World* (1932) and George Orwell's *1984*
(1945), but there were many others that preceded or followed those two.
Utopian Studies includes dystopias and every other kind of topos that
postulates an alternative society.

In the 1970s, there was a new surge of what might be called post-
dystopian utopias. Most of them are considered science fiction novels.
There are ecological utopias such as Ernst Callenbach's *Ecotopia* (1975)
and self-proclaimed heterotopias like Samuel Delany's *Triton* (1976), but
most of the new utopias are feminist. Although some scholars saw these
feminist utopias as something new, feminist scholars went directly to work
to prove that there is a long history of feminist utopias going back to
Margaret Cavendish's *Blazing-World* in 1668. Feminist scholars are
working hard to show a continuity in feminist utopian writing from
Cavendish to the present. The feminist works that receive the most attention include two novels by Ursula K. Le Guin: *The Dispossessed* (1974) and
Always Coming Home (1985). Other Le Guin works are often brought
into utopian discussions as well, since the utopian impulse has always been
strong in Le Guin.

What these various topoi have in common is that they all postulate alternative societies, whether positive or negative. Utopian Studies embraces
both utopian and dystopian literature. This genre is by its nature a socio-
political critique of an author's own society. The comparison may be implicit or explicit, it can be done satirically or in deadly earnestness, but the
comparison is there. An author's vision of utopia fixes whatever he or she
sees as wrong in society. Utopias are in a sense written in reaction to
known societies; dystopias are written sometimes in reaction to utopias
and sometimes as a warning about the direction society is headed.

The relationship between Utopian Studies and science fiction is, to put
it mildly, ambiguous. Some scholars claim that utopian literature is a subgenre of science fiction, while others would have it that science fiction is a
direct descendant of utopian literature. The middle-of-the-road opinion is
that some utopias are science fiction and some are not, depending on
whether or not the work incorporates scientific progress or is set in the
future. *The Dispossessed* and *Always Coming Home* are both utopian literature and science fiction. Both novels are utopian in that they posit alternate societies that are an improvement on our own. *The Dispossessed* is
set far in the future on two alien worlds and concerns a science called
temporal physics, so it is clearly science fiction. *Always Coming Home* generally ignores technological advances, but it is set in the future conditional
on our own planet — about people who "might be going to have lived a

long, long time from now in Northern California," according to Le Guin's introduction ("First Note").

The Dispossessed, which is subtitled *An Ambiguous Utopia*, is set in the Hainish universe several centuries before Le Guin's earlier works. It is the story of a brilliant physicist named Shevek, who lives on a barren and inhospitable planet called Anarres. This planet serves as the moon of a much richer planet, Urras, although it would be more accurate to call these two bodies twin planets. The anarchic society on Anarres is presented as a planned utopia composed of settlers from Urras. As Shevek grows up in this society, he discovers some of its limitations; for instance, anarchic socialism does not foster genius. In order to pursue his scientific studies, he goes to Urras, where he encounters many splendors and also many outrages but manages to complete his temporal theory. Le Guin's previous Hainish novels contain a device called the ansible that allows for instantaneous communications across vast distances of space and without which the League of All Worlds and the Ekumen could not exist; Shevek's temporal theory becomes the basis for the creation of the ansible.

When Le Guin published *The Dispossessed* in 1974, she had several obstacles to overcome. First, there was her own recent success: *The Left Hand of Darkness* had won all the science fiction awards and *The Farthest Shore* had won the National Book Award. A writer's own success can sometimes become her biggest challenge. Secondly, Le Guin had by now been classified as a writer of science fiction and children's fantasy, both of which categories relegated her to the B list of contemporary writers. Thirdly, her science fiction audience held certain expectations based on her previous books; such expectations can hamper an author's wish to experiment. But Le Guin was equal to all these challenges.

The reviews for *The Dispossessed* were largely favorable. The only slight criticism came from James Hamilton-Paterson in the *Times Literary Supplement*, who found the novel too preachy:

> *The Dispossessed* is largely a novel of conversations, often of sixth-form polemics. It is written with thought, care, even love — but its tone is one of unrelieved earnestness. And the notion of an allegory, once planted, is always in the reader's mind, calling attention to itself, a little red flag in one hand, a little blue flag in the other, wildly semaphoring: This Is a Message. (704)

Despite this review in *TLS*, Robert C. Elliott, the preeminent scholar of utopian literature, complained in *The Yale Review* that none of the major review organs gave the book the attention it deserved. He observed that in mainstream journals and magazines it was included in composite reviews of the latest science fiction; only in science fiction magazines did it stand alone. According to Elliott, being classified as science fiction relegated the novel to the science fiction ghetto, whereas it belongs to the great tradition of utopian literature reaching back to Plato: "It is as though Le Guin had set out to test Socrates' contention in *The Republic* that the ideal state is one in which people lead hard, simple lives, producing only necessities" (258). Part of the problem, says Elliott, is that in its quest for literary respectability, science fiction has attempted to subsume utopian literature as a subgenre instead of recognizing it as a separate genre of its own. The association with science fiction has led to the devaluation of utopian literature. Finally, Elliott celebrates *The Dispossessed* for revitalizing a dying genre; he had practically signed the death certificate the year before in an essay on utopian literature.

Ignoring Elliott's complaints, the science fiction community continued to embrace *The Dispossessed* as one of its own. In 1975 the book won both the Hugo and the Nebula awards for best novel of the year, marking the first time any author had won both awards twice. That same year Le Guin's short story "The Day before the Revolution" also won a Nebula. The story is a prequel to *The Dispossessed* about the last day of Odo, the founder of the alternate society that emigrated to Anarres. The tone of both novel and short story is more reminiscent of contemporary realistic fiction than of the romantic quests of Le Guin's earlier science fiction. The short story in particular barely passes as science fiction; it could as easily be taking place in a foreign country as on an alien planet. These two works mark a change in Le Guin's style.

The first scholarly examination of *The Dispossessed* occurred soon after its publication. The Le Guin issue of *Science-Fiction Studies* in November 1975 contained four articles that ostensibly focused on the latest novel. However, the authors of all four articles show more interest in *The Left Hand of Darkness* than in the book they are supposedly discussing. The first of these articles was by Fredric Jameson, now an eminent literary scholar whose penchant for incomprehensible and turgid scholarly prose has earned him several "awards" for bad academic writing. "World-Reduction in Le Guin: The Emergence of Utopian Narrative" is not a model of lucidity. Jameson's interest is in *The Left Hand of Darkness* as a precursor to *The Dispossessed*. He sees signs of the utopian impulse in the earlier work, but both novels operate according to a principle Jameson has just discovered:

a principle of systematic exclusion, a kind of surgical excision of empirical reality, something like a process of ontological attenuation in which the sheer teeming multiplicity of what exists, of what we call reality, is deliberately thinned and weeded out through an operation of radical abstraction and simplification which we will henceforth term world-reduction.

(223)

One of the realities Le Guin strips from Anarres is other animal forms. For Jameson, this suggests that Le Guin is erasing Darwinian determinism to allow humans to create their own destinies. Stripping the Gethenians of gender identity in *Left Hand* was a kind of practice in world-reduction that made possible the creation of an ambiguous utopia in *The Dispossessed* — a utopia stripped of all possessions.

Judah Bierman's "Ambiguity in Utopia: *The Dispossessed*" pays more attention to the titular novel, but Bierman is mostly interested in the book's subtitle, *An Ambiguous Utopia*. What makes it ambiguous, to Bierman, is that Anarres is almost barren of growing things and that the society there discourages creativity and genius. The principles upon which Anarres was founded are utopian, but its practices and its environment can hardly be called ideal.

The third article in the special issue is much quoted by later critics. "The Art of Social-Science Fiction: The Ambiguous Utopian Dialectics of Ursula K. Le Guin," by Donald F. Theall, proposes that most utopian literature is structured according to a dialectical logic that involves both critiquing a modern society and positing an alternative one. In most utopian works, the dialectical mode creates a weakness in the plot because narration is overwhelmed by description of the static utopia. Le Guin avoids that trap by using the storytelling techniques of adventure fantasy, which is strong on plot. Referring to Le Guin's earlier science fiction, Theall says the history and nature of the Ekumen itself reflect utopianism. Le Guin presents the galactic confederation as an ideal, yet she still manages to critique it, especially in *Left Hand*. The earlier Hainish novels are linked to *The Dispossessed* by the unifying theme of communication. This is one reason why Anarres is an ambiguous utopia — it can only remain pure by refusing to communicate with other societies, yet communication is vital to healthy growth.

One interesting point that Theall makes is that the structure of *The Dispossessed* reflects the dialectics of utopian literature: the chapters alternate between Shevek's visit to Urras and flashbacks to his earlier years on Anarres. This structure has obvious connections to Shevek's unified temporal theory as well, which is a dialectic between simultaneity and sequence. Le Guin carries her dialectics through every aspect of her work, including character, showing that ambivalence is just as important to her as balance.

Editor Darko Suvin wrote the final article on *The Dispossessed* for the 1975 special issue of *Science-Fiction Studies*. However, in "Parables of De-Alienation: Le Guin's Widdershins Dance," Suvin pays more attention to Le Guin's other works than to *The Dispossessed*, devoting his special attention to the short story "The New Atlantis," which had just been published in an anthology of the same name. Although Suvin is highly regarded in science fiction circles, this particular article does not provide any amazing new insights into Le Guin's work, probably because editor Suvin was trying to tie in as many of Le Guin's ignored titles as possible to round out his special issue. As a result, the article meanders from one generality to another. Suvin does make the original observation that Le Guin's heroes have evolved from outsiders to "characterological embodiment of the territory" (265), by which he means Shevek is the perfect product of his environment. Le Guin's description of environment has evolved also, so that character and setting are perfectly suited to each other.

Toward the end of his article Suvin comments that Taoism is not the overriding influence some critics want it to be, because after the extremely Taoist *The Lathe of Heaven* Le Guin has moved on to other interests. (I mention this comment particularly because later critics would take exception to it.) The major influences in *The Dispossessed*, which Suvin considers her masterpiece, are "poets from Marvell and Coleridge on, and social novelists from Dickens, Stendhal and Dostoevsky to Soltzhenitsyn and Virginia Woolf" (273). Suvin ranks Le Guin among the top writers of the day, both within and without science fiction. Once again a science fiction scholar is linking Le Guin to canonical authors in order to raise science fiction to a higher level of literary respectability.

Suvin's special issue opened the floodgates for Le Guin criticism in the science fiction journals. Articles on Le Guin became staple fare. The November 1978 issue of *Science-Fiction Studies* included an article by Raymond Williams on "Utopia and Science Fiction." Williams divides utopian texts into four types and their corresponding negatives (dystopias): paradise/hell, a world altered for better or worse by an unexpected natural event, willed transformation (a good or bad change resulting from human effort), technological transformation that improves or worsens life. According to Williams, the first type is never science fiction and, in fact, rarely utopian. The other three types may be either science fiction or utopian literature or both. Williams then turns to a discussion of specific utopian texts. He says that *The Dispossessed* is clearly a return to the traditional utopia, despite the science fiction trappings. On the other hand, it is also a new type of utopian literature that reflects the mores of its time:

In two evident ways, then, *The Dispossessed* has the marks of its period; the wary questioning of the utopian impulse itself, even within its basic acceptance; the uneasy consciousness that the superficies of utopia — affluence and abundance — can be achieved, at least for many, by non-utopian and even anti-utopian means. (213)

Urras, the non-utopia, is the planet that enjoys the good life associated with the classical utopias; utopian Anarres suffers from poverty and famine. So Anarres is not the transformed society so much as a getaway from a corrupt but privileged affluence. Anarres is socially, ethically, morally more highly developed than Urras. Such a reversal of utopian expectations marks the novel as a product of its time. Whereas the classical utopia was static in its perfection, Le Guin's utopia is open to change and self-examination; this questioning of ideals is also symptomatic of the time period in which the novel was written.

Two of the articles in Olander and Greenberg's 1979 collection, *Ursula K. Le Guin*, address *The Dispossessed*. Philip E. Smith's "Unbuilding Walls: Human Nature and the Nature of Evolutionary and Political Theory in *The Dispossessed*" traces the influence of a well-known anarchist, Prince Peter Aledseevich Kropotkin, on Le Guin's ambiguous utopia. Le Guin read many anarchist texts before writing *The Dispossessed*, including works by Kropotkin. Smith shows that Kropotkin's *Mutual Aid* (1902) provides the basis for Le Guin's imagined anarchist community on Anarres. Kropotkin believes mutual aid is a stronger force in evolution than aggression; he sees an evolutionary progression from mutual aid to justice to morality. In *The Dispossessed*, Le Guin shows mutual aid as at least as strong as the will to dominance. On Urras, all the regimes are authoritarian in a way that reflects social Darwinism — aggression and power and centralized authority — whereas Anarres exhibits the morality resulting from applying Kropotkin's ideas about cooperation and personal freedom. According to Smith, Le Guin has not only borrowed Kropotkin's theory, but she has also taken some of his ideas about how such a society would work in practical terms, in providing food, clothing, shelter, education, manufacturing. Le Guin agrees with Kropotkin that the society must remain open rather than becoming static; change is vital to growth. The other major item Le Guin has borrowed from Kropotkin is the image of the wall. This is the binding image of the novel; there are walls, both figurative and literal, in every chapter. Shevek's goal is to tear down the walls that divide people; that was also Kropotkin's goal for an anarchist society.

The second noteworthy utopian article in Olander and Greenberg is "Anarchism and Utopian Tradition in *The Dispossessed*," by John P. Brennan and Michael C. Down. According to these authors, anarchism and utopianism are usually seen as mutually exclusive, but Le Guin has managed to combine them. Brennan and Down make much of Le Guin's title, suggesting that it is connected to Dostoevsky's *The Possessed* (1871–72), a satire on a movement that influenced anarchism. The title also refers to a major tenet of anarchism, freedom from property. Even though the novel is clearly connected to anarchism and utopianism, however, Brennan and Down claim that it is "a penetrating critique of all utopian experience, even that of anarchism, a critique which raises questions that are fundamental to political theory" (117).

According to Brennan and Down, Le Guin has correctly termed her novel "ambiguous," because everything in it features a level of ambiguity. Even the wall in the opening chapter is described as "ambiguous." There is ambiguity about utopia, about other political systems, about values, about physics, about loyalties. Even at the end the novel remains ambiguous, refusing to give answers to the questions it raises. Because of its ambiguity, Brennan and Down claim that *The Dispossessed* doesn't fit into any of the standard narrative types of utopian literature. They then go on to evaluate the society on Anarres according to seven common features of utopian societies. The first feature is that the utopian community generally comes about through revolution; this is certainly true on Anarres. A second feature is that people strive for equality. The equality on Anarres can be seen most clearly when compared to the sexism and social hierarchy on Urras. Thirdly, utopian communities tend to have communal living quarters. Again, on Anarres people live in dorms and eat in large dining areas. Another characteristic of utopias is that they try to erase the dividing line between work and play. This feature is not as obvious on Anarres, where mutuality requires everyone to do occasional grunt work. Utopias also tend to be technologically stable, and Anarres does show restraint in that area. Utopias address the question of urban blight. Not only are there no large cities on Anarres, but since there is no property, there are no ghettos and no crime. Finally, utopias try to reform education. Anarres has a problem in this area, because the anarchists have not been able to balance the needs of the society with the needs of the individual. On the whole, however, to Brennan and Down this analysis proves that according to traditional characteristics Anarres is unambiguously utopian. On the other hand, this utopia becomes ambiguous in the way Le Guin deals with politics and values. Shevek's values are different from those of his society. In most utopias, politics and values are decidedly unambiguous.

The other essay collection of 1979, Joe De Bolt's *Ursula K. Le Guin: Voyager to Inner Lands and to Outer Space*, also contains two articles on *The Dispossessed*. One is by Elizabeth Cummins Cogell, who later wrote the excellent bibliography on Le Guin. "Taoist Configurations: 'The Dispossessed'" objects to Darko Suvin's dismissal of Taoism as a continuing influence on Le Guin, particularly on *The Dispossessed*. Cogell believes that Taoism is the one constant influence on Le Guin and that her work cannot be understood without a knowledge of philosophical Taoism. Rather than growing away from it, Le Guin has continued to delve more and more deeply into Taoism and use it in more complex ways.

Cogell claims that Le Guin uses three primary tenets of Taoism in *The Dispossessed*: "following the model of Nature, the Theory of Letting Alone, and the eternality of change" (154). These tenets can be seen in the areas of science, personal development, society, and government. For Taoists, science is one way to knowledge; Shevek's unified theory of time fits easily into Taoism, involving as it does two apparently contradictory truths about time. Shevek's science reflects two principles of Taoism:

> First, the Taoist recognizes that within one concept or entity is always contained its other, that there are no true opposites but that all possibilities are contained within one . . . . The second Taoist principle on which Shevek's search is founded is that change is eternal, reality is process.
>
> (157)

The concrete analogies used in Taoism are also present in *The Dispossessed*, as is paradox. The form of anarchy practiced on Anarres is closely akin to Taoism. What Cogell calls the Theory of Letting Alone is known in Taoism as *wu wei* — taking no unnecessary action. This form of passive receptivity is practiced on Anarres. Just like Taoists, the anarchists in *The Dispossessed* believe that the individual must develop first in order to be of use to the community. In Cogell's view, by the end of the novel Shevek has developed so much that he is a Taoist sage, having learned by experience the truth of the dictum that the means are the ends.

The second article in the De Bolt volume approaches *The Dispossessed* through sociology. Larry L. Tifft and Dennis C. Sullivan's "Possessed Sociology and Le Guin's *Dispossessed*: From Exile to Anarchism" criticizes modern sociology as being too removed from actual human experience. Sociology does not recognize its own role in perpetuating the "isms" it describes: sexism, racism, ageism, militarism. Anarchism, say these authors, is a form of sociology that includes human experience. Both Shevek and his creator take the risk of reaching out to share their gifts, thus making themselves vulnerable to experience. Tifft and Sullivan show that Shevek has to learn the same lesson of including human experience in his science. He cannot complete his unified theory of time in isolation; communication and exchange are vital. The individual cannot develop fully in isolation. This article is so disorganized that it is difficult to determine its main point. The authors seem to be trying to tie sociology into the understanding of *The Dispossessed*, but their efforts are only partly successful. They also make the mistake of conflating the ideas of the protagonist with those of the author and assuming that every word Shevek speaks reflects the beliefs of his creator.

The special Le Guin issue of *Extrapolation* in Fall of 1980 contains one article of interest to utopian studies. In "Beyond Negation: The Critical Utopias of Ursula K. Le Guin and Samuel R. Delany," Tom Moylan coins the term "critical utopia" to refer to the new utopian literature of the 1970s (what I earlier called "post-dystopian utopias" and some critics have called "open-ended utopias"). Critical utopias can negate, preserve, and transform the utopian tradition. Moylan sees these critical utopias as a natural outgrowth of the social movements of the 1960s and of the maturing of science fiction beyond simple-minded adventures in space. The bulk of his article compares *The Dispossessed* to Delany's *Triton* (1976). As critical utopias, Delany's is more powerful because it preserves, negates, and transforms the utopian mode, whereas Le Guin's novel merely preserves. According to Moylan, the reason why *The Dispossessed* fails to negate and transform is that Le Guin does not really set up a conflict between the individual's needs and those of the community: "The liberty of the individual is joined in dialectical tension with the needs of the society: a nonantagonistic contradiction that provides Anarres with its fundamental human energy" (240). The two sets of needs work together and balance each other. (Moylan seems to have skipped chapter 1 of *The Dispossessed*, in which Shevek faces the threat of being stoned to death by his community.)

Moylan makes two specific criticisms of Le Guin. Even though she sets up her society as nonsexist, her clear preference for partnership and "her de-emphasis of homosexual relations" shows that she "maintains a bias in favor of monogamy and heterosexuality" (241). Moylan, who is more of a marxist than a feminist, has borrowed this criticism from Samuel Delany's *The Jewel-Hinged Jaw* (1977), which contains some harsh criticism of *The Dispossessed* and which seems to have influenced Moylan's perceptions throughout his article. Moylan also thinks that the anarchist ideas that inform the creation of Anarres overshadow the plot of the novel and turn the characters into flat symbols of anarchist ideals. On the whole, Moylan favors *Triton* over *The Dispossessed*, although he tries to point out strengths and weaknesses in both.

In 1981 *The Journal of General Education* published an unusual article by James P. Farrelly, "The Promised Land: Moses, Nearing, Skinner, and Le Guin." According to Farrelly, place is vital in both positive and negative utopian literature: "By their nature, positive utopias demonstrate this 'fortunate union' of people and place, tying character to theme and both to location in a singular image of truth. Negative utopias, on the other hand, tend to distort the truth and to present man as alienated from his environment . . . " (15). Farrelly proposes that both types, negative and positive, descend directly from the model of Moses searching for the Promised Land, then he applies this model to the utopian writers mentioned in his title. Speaking of Le Guin, he says that Shevek plays a Moses role, but he is more a prophet than a leader of his people. Shevek is seeking a promised land for his people — a place that has no walls. Like Moses, he keeps his promise but fails to enter the promised land, although he has blazed the trail for others to follow. As a self-proclaimed congenital non-Christian, Le Guin might object to Farrelly's Christian interpretation of her novel, but the Promised Land as a model for utopia works well.

James Bittner entered the discussion in 1983 with an article entitled "Chronosophy, Aesthetics, and Ethics in Le Guin's *The Dispossessed: An Ambiguous Utopia.*" Bittner's article appeared in an essay collection called *No Place Else: Explorations in Utopian and Dystopian Fiction.* In this essay, Bittner claims that Le Guin transforms the basic utopian question from "Where is utopia?" to "When is utopia?" Since the question concerns time rather than place, *The Dispossessed* is more of a "uchronia" than a utopia. Time is a vital element in the novel: the plot centers around Shevek's search for a unified theory of time, and the structure alternates between Shevek's past and present. Both theme and structure thus transform the novel into a "cyclical sonata form" (247). Bittner draws this musical analogy directly from the book, in which he sees a continual interplay between music and science.

Bittner suggests that the name of the anarchists' founder, Odo, comes from the Greek word *odos*, which can mean many things — road, channel of a river, way to truth, useful, journeying, course of action, way of telling a story. These meanings are all significant for the novel and can be linked to Le Guin's interest in Taoism. Bittner's discussion of all the possible connotations of Odo's name and their significance in the novel may seem like a stretch at first; however, since Le Guin has shown a distinct awareness of such reverberations of meaning in the proper names she invents, Bittner's explication is perhaps not so improbable. On the other hand, when he tries to tie Odo's name to the arrangement of chapters in the novel, his argument becomes convoluted and increasingly incomprehensible, as indeed does his musical analogy.

An important, though opaquely abstract, article on utopia appeared in *Science-Fiction Studies* in 1984. Bulent Somay's "Toward an Open-Ended Utopia" borrows terms from Darko Suvin's theory of science fiction in order to explain utopian literature. Somay uses the terms "utopian locus" and "utopian horizon" to explain the utopian longing that has always existed in humans:

> The *utopian longing* which arose from the people's collective imagination throughout history was thus enclosed in a fictive *utopian locus* which arose from the individual imagination of the author, who presented it to her or his audience in a finished, unchanging, form. What the utopographer did was to verbalize and enclose the *utopian horizon* of an age, which was in itself non-discursive, infinite, and open-ended. (25)

The locus, therefore, is an actual utopian text of any kind. The traditional utopia froze the vision for the writer's culture and time. This allowed dystopian writers to come along later and criticize the vision. To salvage the utopian ideal, the new utopian writers of the 1970s had to disarm the dystopian critics, in so doing creating a new form of utopian writing that Somay calls "open-ended," which "portrays a utopian locus as a mere phase in the infinite unfolding of the utopian horizon" (26). Needless to say, *The Dispossessed* is a prime example of an open-ended utopia. The utopian horizon is present, but it can never be reached, never be frozen in a static vision.

Many of the scholars who followed Somay use this notion of a utopian horizon and locus to discuss Le Guin. Others look instead at her acknowledged feminism. Le Guin's interest in utopia stems from her feminist beliefs, as Deirdre Burton argues in "Linguistic Innovation in Feminist Utopian Fiction," an article that appeared in *Ilha-do-Desterro: A Journal of Language and Literature* in 1985. Burton discusses several feminist utopian writers who have experimented with language in an attempt to imagine language that does not contain patriarchal overtones. The texts Burton examines are Charlotte Perkins Gilman's *Herland* (1915), Marge Piercy's *Woman on the Edge of Time* (1976), Doris Lessing's *The Marriages Between Zones Three, Four and Five* (1980), and Le Guin's *The Dispossessed*. Piercy and Lessing are two authors often compared to Le Guin in terms of their utopian writings; Gilman appears occasionally in Le Guin criticism.

Burton mentions the Sapir-Whorf hypothesis, which states that a culture's language determines its conception of reality. If we want to change the way people think, we must change their language. This is a basic tenet of a branch of feminism. In *The Dispossessed*, Le Guin's anarchists speak an artificially created language called Pravic, which contains and excludes certain concepts from the tongue the settlers spoke before they came to Anarres. Some of the language issues Burton sees in the novel are "swearing; forms of address and politeness phenomena; subject-object relationships; the means for expressing pronouns; honorifics; the means for indicating possession, ownership, sexuality, family relationships, work, play and so on" (90). Some words are slipped into the novel without explanation, so that the reader learns from the context what "egoizing," "profiteer," and "propertarian" mean to the inhabitants of Anarres.

All four of the novels Burton discusses cause a linguistic defamiliarization by questioning assumptions about language, but they do not do it in the same way or to the same extent. Gilman's book creates the least amount of defamiliarization, followed by Le Guin, Piercy, and Lessing. Gilman uses inverted commas to call attention to specific words, an intrusive device that can aid in defamiliarization or irritate the reader, according to Burton. Le Guin approaches language in a more complex way than Gilman; in *The Dispossessed* "the language-reality debate is not only influenced by lexical issues, but by syntax and metaphor as well" (98). However, while Le Guin often interjects linguistic explanations in her novel, Piercy simply throws her invented words and syntax into conversations without explanation so that readers must figure out their meaning from the context. Lessing's book contains the most extreme level of defamiliarization because it never provides the background knowledge necessary to fully comprehend the events in the story.

A 1987 essay collection, *Storm Warnings: Science Fiction Confronts the Future*, contains two articles of interest to utopian criticism of *The Dispossessed*. T. A. Shippey, who had contributed an excellent article to Earthsea criticism, looks at the connection between *The Dispossessed* and George Orwell's *Nineteen Eighty-Four*. "Variations on Newspeak: The Open Question of *Nineteen Eighty-Four*" examines Orwell's use of language control for political purposes. Shippey believes that Le Guin's science fiction engages with Orwell's ideas about Newspeak and doublethink, particularly in "The Word for World Is Forest" and *The Dispossessed*. In the former, Le Guin uses language satire to depict Captain Davidson and Colonel Dongh, both of whom practice doublethink. According to Shippey, *The Dispossessed* attempts to refute Orwell's notion that a thought crime would be impossible without the words to think it in (this goes back to the Sapir-Whorf hypothesis discussed in Deirdre Burton's article). Initially, the reader is led to believe that Pravic, the artificial language on Anarres, has been a complete success. However, even though Pravic does not have words for certain concepts such as possession, those things still exist on Anarres, and although the language tries to excise all ideas of possession, words related to possession are used as insults and swear words. In Shippey's view, Le Guin has constructed Pravic to disprove the idea that language controls thought — the operating principle of Orwell's Newspeak.

The second Le Guin article in *Storm Warnings* is Gregory Benford's "Reactionary Utopias." Benford is a physics professor and a writer of "hard" science fiction, which refers to fiction based on the so-called hard sciences, such as astronomy, biology, physics, and computer science. Technology plays a major role in hard science fiction. Le Guin, on the other hand, is associated with "soft" science fiction because she extrapolates from social sciences like anthropology, ecology, linguistics, and psychology. In soft science fiction, human elements are much more important than technological developments. Practitioners of hard science fiction tend to look down on the soft sciences and, through association, those who write soft science fiction. There is also a political divide: writers of hard science fiction are more likely to be conservative in their political views, while those who employ the social sciences are often liberal. This background helps to explain Benford's rhetorical stance.

Benford believes most utopias are reactionary and regressive in five particular ways: they lack cultural diversity, they are static, they are nostalgic and technophobic, they have an authority figure, and they regulate society through guilt. Benford admits that there are some progressive utopias as well, such as Delany's *Triton*. He loosely associates the reactionary utopias with Europe and the progressive utopias with America. However, he sees Le Guin's *The Dispossessed* as reactionary. Benford's reasons for considering the novel reactionary are somewhat arbitrary. He claims that Anarres has a nineteenth-century "feel" to it, which gives it a static flavor and exhibits Le Guin's "reverence for the European tradition of utopian thought" (75). He also sees the anarchists as technophobic. The guilt Benford has listed as a characteristic of reactionary utopias is seen in *The Dispossessed* in the many Old Testament themes and images (an observation that no doubt surprised the decidedly non-Christian Le Guin). On Anarres guilt is the primary form of social control. Odo, the founder of the revolution, is the authority figure in this reactionary utopia, and Benford identifies Odo with Le Guin herself. Because both Odo and Le Guin are mature women, Benford says, "Living on Anarres has an uncanny resemblance to being nagged by your mother" (76).

Benford accuses Le Guin of avoiding the problems of evil and violence. Even though *The Dispossessed* includes scenes of street confrontation on Urras, the scenes don't ring true: "So her anarchists, confronting theory rather than facts, come over as nice, reasonable, and fairly boring. They behave like middle-class middle-brows, except that they are scrupulously horrified at the idea of property" (79). Benford then accuses Le Guin of disliking cultural diversity, which is a peculiar charge to bring against an author who has always quietly placed her protagonists in ethnic groups considered minorities. To make this charge, Benford has to call upon evidence from an essay by Samuel Delany, "To Read *The Dispossessed*," a rambling, self-indulgent essay in Delany's *The Jewel-Hinged Jaw*. Like Benford, Delany is both an academic and a science fiction writer. Delany seems to think that Le Guin dislikes homosexuals because she has Shevek give up a homosexual affair for a long-term heterosexual partnership. From Delany's less-than-logical interpretation, Benford leaps to the conclusion that since Le Guin favors a marriage-type relationship for her protagonist, she clearly dislikes cultural diversity.

The real target of Benford's invective is feminist utopias in general, as becomes obvious by the end of his article. Le Guin's novel is simply a handy representative of the breed. Feminists, says Benford, always overlook the need for control in their utopias, probably because they have so little experience in the real world, which is highly competitive. They are all reacting to perceived (and imaginary) masculine evils. All the writers Benford lists as successful at portraying realistic human beings in utopian surroundings are, needless to say, men. The only person who truly comes across as reactionary in this article about reactionary utopias is Benford himself. Since *Storm Warnings* was published in 1987, Benford could easily have read Le Guin's latest utopian offering, *Always Coming Home* (1985), before he wrote his article. That would explain his anti-feminist rhetoric better than a reading of *The Dispossessed* would. After all, *The Dispossessed* is a man's story and presents its utopia as ambiguous.

The strong connection between Le Guin's utopianism and feminism became blatantly obvious with the publication of *Always Coming Home*. At Le Guin's insistence, the publisher called this illustrated book a novel, but it is like no novel ever seen. It is more like a folklore encyclopedia of the Kesh people, a tribe-like group of people living in California in the far future. There are poems, stories, songs, maps, charts, histories, lists, illustrations, even footprints. The illustrations and graphics were provided by illustrator Margaret Chodos. The deluxe version of the book came with a cassette tape of Kesh songs and poetry, with music composed by Todd Barton. Rather than a novel, *Always Coming Home* is a multimedia event. The book isn't even organized in any kind of standard fashion: all the elements are mixed together in a carefully planned hodge-podge that results in the acknowledgments appearing as what could be considered the last chapter, "Pandora No Longer Worrying."

Le Guin had been reading and thinking a lot since 1974, when *The Dispossessed* appeared. The ideas she had been thinking about are best expressed in a 1982 lecture in honor of Robert C. Elliott, the historian of utopian literature. As published in Le Guin's essay collection *Dancing at the Edge of the World*, the lecture is entitled "A Non-Euclidean View of California as a Cold Place to Be." Using her knowledge of the ancient

Native American cultures in California, Le Guin shows that the traditional approach to utopia is linear, rational, masculine, euclidean, European. She proposes an alternative — a utopia that would be based on process rather than progress. As Le Guin explains,

> Utopia has been yang. In one way or another, from Plato on, utopia has been the big yang motorcycle trip. Bright, dry, clear, strong, firm, active, aggressive, lineal, progressive, creative, expanding, advancing, and hot . . . . What would a yin utopia be? It would be dark, wet, obscure, weak, yielding, passive, participatory, circular, cyclical, peaceful, nurturant, retreating, contracting, and cold. (90)

Le Guin borrows the terms "hot" and "cold" from Claude Lévi-Strauss, who differentiates societies in this way. She admits that *The Dispossessed* is mostly a yang utopia, although the anarchism propounded in the novel is "about as yin as a political ideology can get" (93). The essay makes it clear that she was now thinking along different lines about utopia. *Always Coming Home* is the result of that change of perception.

Reviewers responded with more open-mindedness than might be expected. Since many reviews tend to summarize the basic plots of novels and it is impossible to summarize a nonexistent plot, reviewers could easily have thrown up their hands in despair when faced with *Always Coming Home*. On the contrary, however, most reviewers were generous. Samuel R. Delany, who had been one of the harshest critics of *The Dispossessed*, wrote a glowing review of *Always Coming Home* for the *New York Times Book Review*. He called it Le Guin's "most consistently lyric and luminous book" (31). The only thing that irritated Le Guin about the early reviews was a tendency on the part of some reviewers to assume that the Kesh live in a post-nuclear-holocaust world. Brian Aldiss, a well-known British science fiction writer, makes this assumption in his review for the *Washington Post*, as does Peter S. Prescott in *Newsweek*. *Always Coming Home* does not even hint at nuclear destruction, so these reviewers are reading something into the novel that was never intended.

For at least one science fiction writer, however, *Always Coming Home* was the last straw. Norman Spinrad, writing a column for *Isaac Asimov's Science Fiction Magazine* in 1986, attacked the book with an excess of venom. Venom was nothing new coming from Spinrad. He had been an angry young man in the 1960s, writing novels that seemed to deliberately provoke offense through their linguistic and sexual frankness. When *Bug Jack Barron* (1969) was serialized in a British science fiction magazine, many bookstores in Britain banned the magazine. Spinrad had maintained his anger into his more mature years, so his column was not a model of gentility. Usually, however, Spinrad chose as targets ultraconservative beliefs and values, as befits a former sixties rebel, not the work of liberal friends like Le Guin.

Most of Spinrad's article is a complaint about the fact that science fiction is ignored by "the established American critical apparatus" because it is supposedly inferior literature. Deriding critics who acclaim a bad science fiction book as great literature merely because it is written by someone from the literary establishment and not labeled "science fiction," Spinrad nevertheless saves most of his invective for "any science fiction writer of merit who is adopted as a 'token nigger' in the grand high salons of literary power and allows ignorant praise to influence the work itself" (9). By this he means Ursula K. Le Guin and *Always Coming Home.* Spinrad accuses Le Guin of writing down to the literary critics who don't understand science fiction, trying to please her intellectual admirers. Winning the National Book Award for *The Farthest Shore* was Le Guin's "passport to higher literary realms" (10). As far as Spinrad is concerned, *The Dispossessed* was Le Guin's last true science fiction novel. Since then her work has devolved into a "political cartoon . . . between evil yang (militarism, technology, male dominance, capitalism, Faustian philosophical activism) and virtuous yin (passivity, ecotopia, socialism, decentralization, the noble granola-eating natural woman)" (11).

In other words, Spinrad believes that Le Guin has sold out to mainstream literature, which is what the science fiction community had feared for years, and as a result "she has lost the creative center, sense of irony, and intellectual discipline that every would-be visionary writer must retain if she is not to devolve into a hectoring guru" (12). He dismisses *Always Coming Home* as "an enormous act of ego-tripping self indulgence" (12). Spinrad clearly identifies with the yang elements he perceives Le Guin to be attacking. His tone is extremely defensive as well as accusatory. Apparently his attitude hadn't changed four years later when he reprinted this column as the first chapter in his book *Science Fiction in the Real World.* As for the hectoring guru, the noble granola-eating natural woman, the token nigger of the literary establishment, she responded with incredible restraint in a letter to the editor. Her letter was a polite reassurance that she does indeed still consider herself a science fiction writer. She signed the letter "Granola Eating Woman."

One of the first scholarly articles on *Always Coming Home* was J. R. Wytenbroek's "*Always Coming Home*: Pacificism [*sic*] and Anarchy in Le Guin's Latest Utopia" in the Winter 1987 issue of *Extrapolation.* This piece seems more like a review essay than an academic analysis, but the author makes a few interesting points. For one thing, Wytenbroek points out how well it works for Le Guin to introduce the Kesh first so that the reader sees other groups from their perspective, particularly the warlike

Condor people. Because the Condor resemble modern American society, this is an excellent way to grant a reader enough distance to see American culture more clearly. Wytenbroek seems to think *Always Coming Home* is more about the Condor than the Kesh — a study of a warlike culture seen from within and without. In order to come to this conclusion, Wytenbroek has to ignore most of the book and concentrate on the chapters dealing with Stone Telling, daughter of a Kesh woman and a Condor man. The Stone Telling chapters are the closest thing to a narrative in *Always Coming Home*, so reviewers and scholars both tend to focus on those sections, even though they constitute at most one-fifth of the book.

Naomi Jacobs has a better understanding of the book than Wytenbroek. Her article, "Beyond Stasis and Symmetry: Lessing, Le Guin, and the Remodeling of Utopia," also appeared in *Extrapolation*, this time in the Spring 1988 issue. Jacobs is interested in how Lessing and Le Guin break the stasis of the classical utopia. By stasis, she not only means that utopia is frozen in time but that the narrative is also static and uninteresting. In *The Marriages Between Zones Three, Four and Five* and *Always Coming Home*, Lessing and Le Guin have created dynamic utopias. *Always Coming Home* abandons the linear narrative Le Guin used in *The Dispossessed*, which Jacobs sees as an example of the Euclidean utopia Le Guin described in "A Non-Euclidean View of California as a Cold Place to Be." Jacobs describes Le Guin's new narrative method as "the complex, multimedia collecting and recording techniques of cultural anthropology" (41). According to Jacobs, this book cannot even be read in a linear fashion but must rather be browsed. Jacobs pays particular attention to the figure of Pandora, the writer-archeologist who is supposedly collecting the material about the Kesh that makes up the book. Through Pandora's seemingly random appearances and interjections, Le Guin destabilizes her text further. Pandora knows she cannot create utopia on her own: she needs the help of readers and of the Kesh themselves. Pandora jumps in and out of the text at will, commenting and participating and exploring the whole process of creating a utopia.

Another feminist writing about *Always Coming Home*, Lee Cullen Khanna, acclaims it as Le Guin's most brilliant work. Khanna speaks with the authority of one who has done extensive research and study in feminist utopian writing. In "Women's Utopias: New Worlds, New Texts" in *Feminism, Utopia, and Narrative* (1990), Khanna compares Le Guin to Thomas More. Both authors employ maps, an invented language, and a playful tone. But Le Guin has improved on More's vision. Khanna points out that the Kesh, though supposedly primitive, have advanced technology. (This comment could be a direct response to those reviewers and critics who complain about technophobic utopias.) Khanna also indicates that Le Guin could be drawing on advances in narrative form and structure that other feminist utopian writers have been inventing — authors such as Marge Piercy and Doris Lessing. Nevertheless, *Always Coming Home* is something entirely new. It seems to deconstruct itself even as Le Guin is creating it. For example, Pandora mentions the difficulties of translating a language that does not exist. Khanna values this aspect of the text: "This undercutting of reality, in the midst of precise detail about the utopian world, invites the reader to see the text as a game and to participate in the creative process" (133).

Le Guin usually employs one or more central images in her works, such as the wall imagery in *The Dispossessed*. The two key images in *Always Coming Home*, says Khanna, are the messy scrub oak and the broken clay pot. Both symbolize the unusual structure of the book. The scrub oak can also refer to the frailty of human nature, which may not be ideally suited to utopia. Like Jacobs, Khanna appreciates the nonlinear structure of the book, which defies a linear reading: "This fractured structure well may foster a rich diversity of reading experiences, and, in contrast to the didactic impulse so common in utopian fiction, invite readers to make multiple meanings" (133). In a similar fashion, the direct address of Pandora involves the reader in the text too.

Another article in *Feminism, Utopia, and Narrative* that touches on *Always Coming Home* is Peter Fitting's "The Turn from Utopia in Recent Feminist Fiction." Fitting claims that the feminist utopias of the 1970s have been replaced in the eighties by a new pessimism about the future, resulting in novels that perceive the future as a dismal reestablishment of brutal repression of women. Fitting's exemplars are Margaret Atwood's *The Handmaid's Tale* (1985), Suzette Haden Elgin's *Native Tongue* (1984), Zoe Fairbairns's *Benefits* (1979), and *Always Coming Home*. Le Guin's book is an exception to the pessimism, but Fitting claims that it too is a retreat from earlier feminist utopianism. The problem Fitting sees in the book is that it never explains how to get from here to there — how such a utopia is supposed to have come about. Of what use is a feminist utopia that can't be reached? The feminist utopias of the 1970s, including *The Dispossessed*, were quite clear about the genesis of their perfect societies.

In 1991 *Science-Fiction Studies* published an article by Jim Jose that returns to the subject of form and content in Le Guin's works, "Reflections on the Politics of Le Guin's Narrative Shifts." Like other critics before him, Jose sees a congruence between the structure of Le Guin's books and the content; however, Jose is interested in tracking the changes in that relationship. He sees the major shift beginning with the short story "The Day Before the Revolution," which shows that Le Guin was already

becoming uncomfortable with the narrative certainty of the recently published *The Dispossessed*. By *Always Coming Home*, the shift is obvious.

Jose says that Le Guin is interested in engaging readers as collaborators
in the creative process. This can be a problem in utopian writing, because
utopian visions are usually exclusionary. Le Guin's narrative shifts are an
attempt to solve this problem. In her early works Le Guin uses a conventional narrative structure — a journey, seen from one main character's
point of view, with a beginning and an end and a purpose that is achieved.
Even *The Dispossessed* fits this structure, despite having alternating chapters
in different time periods. *Always Coming Home* goes a great way toward
solving the problem. Jose is careful to point out that in her latest work
Le Guin is not rejecting the father tongue of patriarchy in favor of a feminist mother tongue, but is rather trying to use both. Most utopian texts
are written in the father tongue, the language of power. Le Guin does not
want language to exclude anyone from utopia. Because of this use of language, the multiplicity of voices, and the fragmented structure, the utopian vision is perfectly represented by the structure of the book. Le Guin
may be the first person to have created an inhabitable utopia.

In 1992 Mario Klarer brought up the topic of *The Dispossessed* again
for an article in *Mosaic*, "Gender and the Simultaneity Principle: Ursula
Le Guin's *The Dispossessed*." Klarer's thesis is that early feminist critiques of
Le Guin are obsolete in the light of more recent feminist scholarship, particularly the work of Monique Witting, "where the emphasis is on syntax,
language and structure and their relationship to socio-cultural, physio-
sexual, or genetic issues" (108). According to Klarer, *The Dispossessed* incorporates and predates these new feminist concerns, which would make
Le Guin a forerunner of contemporary feminist theory. He claims that the
repression of Shevek's work on Anarres fits into "the twofold structure of
women's discourse described by Sandra Gilbert and Susan Gubar" (109).
Shevek has to be conversant with the dominant (patriarchal) discourse in
order to write anything at all, but he also has to subvert that discourse.
Following the lead of James W. Bittner, Klarer compares Le Guin to
Shevek along similar lines: "Her novels simultaneously accord with the
traditional male conventions of science fiction and the utopian novel but
at the same time subvert and revive these conventions through the 'female
voice'" (109).

Klarer says that Le Guin has chosen metaphors and motifs that reflect
the structure of the narrative (the alternating chapters set in past or present, on Anarres or Urras). He lists these motifs as "mobiles, planetary imagery, sexual intercourse, bisexuality, and music" (110), but he perceives
Takver's mobiles as the ideal representation:

The book is structured in concentric circles that oscillate between Urras and Anarres, i.e., time and space, which are also the two structural parameters of Takver's mobiles. Inside each circular string of narrative, Le Guin follows a linear, sequential structure that starts in the past and leads into the future. The description of the mobile thus functions as a graphic rendering of the concentric format of the novel itself. (111)

This narrative structure also reflects Shevek's unified theory of time, which combines simultaneity and sequence. Shevek's theory of time is the same as Le Guin's theory of science fiction. Klarer points out that Le Guin predates the ideas of Julia Kristeva in seeing time as having two interdependent aspects. In a 1981 article, Kristeva associates linear time with patriarchy and says that modern feminists reject linear time in favor of cyclical time. Kristeva also posits an eventual conjoining of the two perceptions of time. These ideas are clearly expressed in *The Dispossessed*, which was written seven years earlier.

The most perceptive criticism of *Always Coming Home* is an article from 1993, "Spiraling around the Hinge: Working Solutions in *Always Coming Home*," by Mary Catherine Harper. This piece appeared in a collection of essays called *Old West-New West: Centennial Essays*. Harper claims that in *Always Coming Home* Le Guin has switched from a unity-in-opposition principle to the process orientation she had described in "A Non-Euclidean View of California as a Cold Place to Be." As Harper explains it,

> *Always Coming Home* contains a personal vision of life where one may refuse to participate in either/or thinking, where one may refuse the cultural dualisms that Americans find themselves trapped in today. This cross-genre "novel" significantly places what we see as opposites — backward and forward — in dialogue with each other. It is a dialogue between American "binarism" and the thought or possibility of an other-than-binary life. (241–42)

The recurring image of the hinge in *Always Coming Home* is a graphic representation of this dialogue and of the concept of centrality, says Harper. This hinge, which Le Guin calls a "heyiya-if," is a modified yin/yang symbol — a basically circular shape that is left open and always presented in a slightly different spiral form. Le Guin describes it as a non-connected double spiral. This symbol, Harper states, "is somewhat contrary to the traditional, fully connected yin-yang symbol. As such, it suggests open-endedness, flexibility in the relationship between its halves, and gradual change rather than unity in opposition" (247). The hinge symbol reappears continuously in *Always Coming Home* in all of the various bits and pieces of text that make up the whole. There are hinged drawings in the songs, charts, maps, histories, descriptions, and even in the structure of the Kesh towns. Harper sees the Kesh themselves as one of these hinges. Pandora indicates that the Kesh have no historical existence. However, they are in many ways representative of ancient Native Americans of the West Coast, and they are also supposedly a future culture. Thus, they operate as a hinge between past and future. Harper gives example after example of how the hinge works in Kesh science, poetry, spirituality, ceremonies, and intellectual concepts. Pandora's anthropological insertions act as a hinge for the entire book.

Unfortunately, not all scholarly criticism is as good as Harper's. A recent trend in Le Guin criticism is to tie her to ecofeminism, and the ecofeminist scholars who have chosen to write about Le Guin are somewhat jargon-ridden. According to the ideas of ecofeminism, a patriarchal society conquers nature and oppresses it in a manner similar to the way women are oppressed and silenced. In *Literature, Nature, and Other: Ecofeminist Critiques*, Patrick D. Murphy claims that *Always Coming Home* is an ecofeminist utopia. This 1995 publication sets Le Guin up as the standard against which ecofeminist writers can be measured. Murphy even examines Le Guin's poetry for ecofeminist echoes. Patrick Murphy is the only critic who has written about Le Guin's poetry, having published two articles specifically on the poems. His attempts to incorporate the poetry into scholarly discourse about Le Guin are admirable. Unfortunately, his opaque style detracts from any insights his studies might provide. For example, in *Literature, Nature and Other* he writes:

> [I]f we conceptualize a three-dimensional playing field along the lines of plate tectonics, consisting of zones of ideological positions arising from and in turn affecting specific historical conditions (the majority of them manifestations of the dominant culture), with interzonal gaps, fissures, fault lines, and impact points, and perceive this diachronically — adding the fourth dimension — then we can locate chronotopes for agency, shifting pivot points in which disruption can transform into eruption, and negation into affirmation. (113)

Le Guin's excursions into utopia have prompted much critical debate, but it seems to have tapered off in the 1990s. Le Guin herself has gone on to other interests and other literary experiments, so utopian critics have not had any new cud to chew on. To date utopian criticism remains in the hands of the ecofeminists. After *Always Coming Home*, Le Guin returned to more traditional modes of storytelling, although she continued to incorporate feminist ideas in her work.

Works Cited

Aldiss, Brian. Rev. of *Always Coming Home*. *Washington Post* (Book World) 6 October 1985: 11.

Benford, Gregory. "Reactionary Utopias." *Storm Warnings: Science Fiction Confronts the Future*. Ed. George E. Slusser, Colin Greenland, and Eric S. Rabkin. Carbondale: Southern Illinois UP, 1987. 73–83.

Bierman, Judah. "Ambiguity in Utopia: *The Dispossessed*." *Science-Fiction Studies* 2 (November 1975): 249–55.

Bittner, James W. "Chronosophy, Aesthetics, and Ethics in Le Guin's *The Dispossessed: An Ambiguous Utopia*." *No Place Else: Explorations in Utopian and Dystopian Fiction*. Ed. Eric S. Rabkin, Martin H. Greenberg, and Joseph D. Olander. Carbondale: Southern Illinois UP, 1983. 244–70.

Brennan, John P., and Michael C. Downs. "Anarchism and Utopian Tradition in *The Dispossessed*. *Ursula K. Le Guin*. Ed. Joseph D. Olander and Martin Harry Greenberg. Writers of the 21st Century Series. New York: Taplinger, 1979. 97–115.

Burton, Deidre. "Linguistic Innovation in Feminist Utopian Fiction." *Ilha-do-Desterro: A Journal of Language and Literature* 14.2 (1985): 82–106.

Cogell, Elizabeth Cummins. "Taoist Configurations: 'The Dispossessed.'" *Ursula K. Le Guin: Voyager to Inner Lands and to Outer Space*. Ed. Joe De Bolt. Literary Criticism Series. Port Washington, NY: Kennikat Press, 1979. 153–79.

Delany, Samuel R. Rev. of *Always Coming Home*. *New York Times Book Review* 29 September 1985: 31–32.

——. "To Read *The Dispossessed*." *The Jewel-Hinged Jaw: Notes on the Language of Science Fiction*. Elizabethtown, NY: Dragon Press, 1977. 239–308.

Elliott, Robert C. "A New Utopian Novel." Rev. of *The Dispossessed*. *Yale Review* 65 (Winter 1976): 256–61.

Farrelly, James P. "The Promised Land: Moses, Nearing, Skinner, and Le Guin." *JGE: The Journal of General Education* 33 (Spring 1981): 15–23.

Fitting, Peter. "The Turn from Utopia in Recent Feminist Fiction." *Feminism, Utopia, and Narrative*. Ed. Libby Falk Jones and Sarah Webster Goodwin. Tennessee Studies in Literature 32. Knoxville: U of Tennessee P, 1990. 141–58.

Hamilton-Paterson, James. "Allegorical Imperatives." Rev. of *The Dispossessed*. *Times Literary Supplement* 20 June 1975: 704.

Harper, Mary Catherine. "Spiraling around the Hinge: Working Solutions in *Always Coming Home*." *Old West-New West: Centennial Essays*. Ed. Barbara Howard Meldrum. Moscow: U of Idaho P, 1993. 241–57.

Jacobs, Naomi. "Beyond Stasis and Symmetry: Lessing, Le Guin, and the Re-modeling of Utopia." *Extrapolation* 29 (Spring 1988): 34–45.

Jameson, Fredric. "World-Reduction in Le Guin: The Emergence of Utopian Narrative." *Science-Fiction Studies* 2 (November 1975): 221–30.

Jose, Jim. "Reflections on the Politics of Le Guin's Narrative Shifts." *Science-Fiction Studies* 18 (1991): 180–97.

Khanna, Lee Cullen. "Women's Utopias: New Worlds, New Texts." *Feminism, Utopia, and Narrative*. Ed. Libby Falk Jones and Sarah Webster Goodwin. Tennessee Studies in Literature 32. Knoxville: U of Tennessee P, 1990. 130–40.

Klarer, Mario. "Gender and the Simultaneity Principle: Ursula Le Guin's *The Dispossessed*." *Mosaic* 25 (Spring 1992): 107–121.

Le Guin, Ursula K. *Always Coming Home*. New York: Harper & Row, 1985.

——. "The Day Before the Revolution." *Galaxy* 35 (August 1974): 17–30.

——. *The Dispossessed*. New York: Harper & Row, 1974.

——. *The Lathe of Heaven*. New York: Scribner's, 1971.

——. Letter to the editor. *Isaac Asimov's Science Fiction Magazine* (April 1987): 14.

——. "The New Atlantis." *The New Atlantis and Other Novellas of Science Fiction*. Ed. Robert Silverberg. New York: Hawthorn, 1975. 57–86.

——. "A Non-Euclidean View of California as a Cold Place to Be." *Dancing at the Edge of the World: Thoughts on Words, Women, Places*. Grove Press, 1989. New York: Harper & Row, 1990. 80–100.

——. "The Word for World Is Forest." *Again, Dangerous Visions*. Ed. Harlan Ellison. Garden City: Doubleday, 1972. 30–108.

Moylan, Tom. "Beyond Negation: The Critical Utopias of Ursula K. Le Guin and Samuel R. Delany." *Extrapolation* 21 (Fall 1980): 236–53.

Murphy, Patrick D. "The Left Hand of Fabulation: The Poetry of Ursula K. Le Guin." *The Poetic Fantastic: Studies in an Evolving Genre*. Ed. Patrick D. Murphy and Vernon Hyles. Contributions to the Study of Science Fiction and Fantasy 40. Westport, CT: Greenwood Press, 1989. 123–36.

——. *Literature, Nature, and Other: Ecofeminist Critiques*. Albany: State U of New York P, 1995.

——. "Robinson Jeffers's Influence on Ursula K. Le Guin." *Robinson Jeffers Newsletter* 72 (March 1988): 20–22.

Prescott, Peter S. Rev. of *Always Coming Home*. *Newsweek* 18 November 1985: 101.

Shippey, T. A. "Variations on Newspeak: The Open Question of *Nineteen Eighty-Four*." *Storm Warnings: Science Fiction Confronts the Future*. Ed. George E. Slusser, Colin Greenwood, and Eric S. Rabkin. Carbondale: Southern Illinois P, 1987. 172–93.

Smith, Philip E., II. "Unbuilding Walls: Human Nature and the Nature of Evolutionary and Political Theory in *The Dispossessed*. *Ursula K. Le Guin*. Ed. Joseph D. Olander and Martin Harry Greenberg. Writers of the 21st Century Series. New York: Taplinger, 1979. 77–96.

Somay, Bulent. "Towards an Open-Ended Utopia." *Science-Fiction Studies* 11 (March 1984): 25–38.

Spinrad, Norman. "Critical Standards." *Isaac Asimov's Science Fiction Magazine* (1986). *Science Fiction in the Real World*. Carbondale: Southern Illinois UP, 1990. 3–17.

Suvin, Darko. "Parables of De-Alienation: Le Guin's Widdershins Dance." *Science-Fiction Studies* 2 (November 1975): 265–74.

Theall, Donald F. "The Art of Social-Science Fiction: The Ambiguous Utopian Dialects of Ursula K. Le Guin." *Science-Fiction Studies* 2 (November 1975): 256–64.

Tifft, Larry L., and Dennis C. Sullivan. "Possessed Sociology and Le Guin's *Dispossessed*: From Exile to Anarchism." *Ursula K. Le Guin: Voyager to Inner Lands and to Outer Space*. Ed. Joe De Bolt. Literary Criticism Series. Port Washington, NY: Kennikat Press, 1979. 180–97.

Williams, Raymond. "Utopia and Science Fiction." *Science-Fiction Studies* 5 (November 1978): 203–14.

Wytenbroek, J. R. "*Always Coming Home*: Pacificism [*sic*] and Anarchy in Le Guin's Utopia." *Extrapolation* 28 (Winter 1987): 330–39.

4: The Carrier Bag

IF I THOUGHT MY EDITOR WOULD LET ME get away with it, I would call this chapter "The Kitchen Sink." However, I have opted for the more Le Guinian title "The Carrier Bag." In a 1986 essay called "The Carrier Bag Theory of Fiction," Le Guin proposes that just as a carrier bag was more useful than a weapon in prehistoric societies, it is also a better model for narrative than is the linear arrow or spear. The arrow is just one possibility (a straight chronological one), whereas the carrier bag can hold many other options. This is my carrier bag chapter. It contains many loosely connected tidbits of Le Guiniana. Its goals are fourfold: 1) to examine the most recent Le Guin criticism, 2) to discuss the many books that have been ignored by critics, 3) to gather together the odds and ends of criticism that are too sparse to rate their own chapters, and 4) to provide a concluding overview of the critical developments from 1966 to 1998. In accordance with Le Guin's preference for circularity, I will discuss these topics in the distinctly non-chronological order listed above.

For the most part, Le Guin criticism today remains divided between science fiction and children's literature. One difference now is that science fiction critics don't view children's literature quite as condescendingly as they used to. Many would disagree with that opinion, particularly academics who practice in both fields, but it seems to me that these scholars are too involved in tree counting to realize the forest has changed. Admittedly, some old trees still boast a thick covering of moss; as recently as 1992 science fiction writer Thomas Disch wrote a scathing article for the *Atlantic Monthly* denouncing bad science fiction as children's literature. He apparently took it for granted that calling anything "children's literature" was a dreadful insult. However, Disch has become one of the dinosaurs he criticizes in his article; most modern critics no longer dismiss children's books as a lesser form of literature. While children's literature and science fiction may not yet hold out open arms to each other, they cross paths more and more often. Children's literature conferences have sessions on science fiction and vice versa. A recent issue of the science fiction journal *Foundation* was devoted entirely to science fiction for young readers. Both fields have matured since the early days of Le Guin criticism, so recent articles generally display more rigorous scholarship and better writing skills than much of the early commentary.

Articles about Le Guin in more mainstream literary journals still crop up here and there, as they have always done. Since the writers of articles in *English Studies* or *Studies in Short Fiction* tend to rediscover insights previously made in a science fiction or children's literature journal, they have not been fairly represented in this book; however, their numbers are growing. Likewise, articles in essay collections are appearing more often, and apprentice scholars continue to write master's theses and doctoral dissertations on aspects of Le Guin's work. Unpublished conference papers on Le Guin would fill several file cabinets, and no one could begin to count the student essays that have been written about her.

The most recent controversy in Le Guin criticism centers around the unexpected appearance in 1990 of a fourth book about Earthsea, *Tehanu: The Last Book of Earthsea*. This was eighteen years after Le Guin had supposedly finished the series — eighteen years during which the author had undergone a sea change in her thinking about issues both political and literary. *Tehanu* is very different from its predecessors. Le Guin picks up the story where she left off, with the supposed restoration of magic in Earthsea by Ged's self-sacrifice. Now, however, the story centers on Tenar, the heroine from *The Tombs of Atuan*, who is a middle-aged widow living on the island of Ged's birth. Tenar adopts an abused and maimed child and nurses a returned Ged back to physical health. While Ged tries to accept the loss of his wizard's power and learn how to live like a normal human, Tenar deals with women's issues — how women's magic is derided by the all-male wizards, how women are victimized and degraded in Earthsea, how to help her adopted daughter become whole. In the end, it is the child who saves Tenar and Ged from an insane wizard by calling for the dragon who is her progenitor.

Many people had requested another book about Earthsea, but *Tehanu* wasn't quite what they had expected. Although a fantasy, many of the scenes are grittily realistic, and the subject matter could be taken from contemporary headlines. *Tehanu* is not at all like the other three books of Earthsea. Its ideal reader is not an adolescent or a child, and things taken for granted in the earlier books are questioned here. Is male wizardry really in control of the Equilibrium? Is a high king really the answer to all of Earthsea's problems? Did Ged's heroic act in *The Farthest Shore* really cure what was ailing Earthsea?

Despite Le Guin's new approach to her fantasy world, most reviews were positive, the only noticeable complaint being that the subtitle of *Tehanu* was *The Last Book of Earthsea*. The reviewers wanted more sequels. Reviewers did have difficulty classifying the novel. The *New York Times Book Review* asked Robin McKinley, a Newbery-winning children's author, to review the book as children's literature, but as she asserts in her review, *Tehanu* is not a children's book. But McKinley was pleased to review the book anyway. She praises Le Guin for her ability to to grow and change:

> The very best thing about this novel is its sense of growth, of distance traveled as well as time passed. The Earthsea trilogy is deservedly considered a classic. Ursula Le Guin shows courage in writing a sequel to an accomplished series that demonstrated the full but traditional intellectual and magical gifts of wizards who were always male. The astonishing clear-sightedness of "Tehanu" is in its recognition of the necessary and life-giving contributions of female magic — sometimes disguised as domesticity.

However, there were a few negative notes. In the *Washington Post* review, Michael Dirda complains that the male characters in the book are all weak, evil, and/or stupid. He also describes the novel as building to a climax "of almost pornographic horror." John Clute, reviewing the novel for the *Times Literary Supplement*, could find nothing positive to say. For Clute, the Earthsea books had been perfect as a trilogy and the new volume is an unwanted feminist intrusion. According to Clute, "The first half of *Tehanu* is a forcible — and at times decidedly bad-tempered — deconstruction of its predecessors." Clute claims that the book has a sour effect on readers, and his conclusion is that "in the end one resents the corrosiveness of *Tehanu*, for in telling this particular tale Le Guin has chosen to punish her own readers for having loved other books she herself wrote."

Le Guin was unhappy about these reviews because she felt that the reviewers did not understand what she was trying to do in *Tehanu*. The criticism bothered her so much that she responded to it in a lecture given at a children's literature conference at Oxford in 1992. The lecture was later published as a pamphlet called *Earthsea Revisioned*. In Western hero-tales, Le Guin says, the hero is always male, and that is why she began her Earthsea books by writing about a male hero — in the 1960s she had not yet realized there were other options. Even then, however, she was subversive to a certain degree in making her heroes dark-skinned. After she finished *The Farthest Shore*, she knew there had to be another book about Earthsea, but she couldn't write it then. She couldn't write it until she had struggled through the changes feminism demanded of her. She wanted to write a book about Earthsea that wasn't also about power and about going on great quests; she wanted to show that a woman's world and a woman's choices are important in their own right. In this essay Le Guin responds to the negative reviews by first contradicting the idea that all the male characters are weak or evil. There are good men in the book, but their virtues are not the ones associated with the traditional hero. As Le Guin puts it, "Traditional masculinists don't want heroism revised and unrewarded. They don't want to find it among housewives and elderly goat-herds. And they really don't want their hero fooling around with grown women" (14–15). The traditional concept of the hero is simply another Western myth — a construct that can be altered as required. Le Guin's essay is intelligent, well-informed, and persuasive, but I suspect it reached mainly an audience of like-minded feminists. Perhaps when it is included in her next published collection of essays, it will reach a wider audience.

As the last book of Earthsea, *Tehanu* received notice from both children's literature critics and the science fiction community. It won the Nebula award for best novel of 1990, establishing Le Guin as the only three-time winner of that honor. Despite being a fantasy rather than a science fiction novel, *Tehanu* was eligible for the Nebula because the Science Fiction Writers of America had expanded to include fantasy writers as well. Within five years of its publication, *Tehanu* was featured in two articles in the highly esteemed annual *Children's Literature*. The first article, by Len Hatfield, came out in 1993. According to Hatfield, Le Guin has been criticizing patriarchy all along, implicitly in the first three books of Earthsea, explicitly in *Tehanu*. Le Guin sees that the marginalization of children is similar to that of women, so *Tehanu* deals with both. As Hatfield indicates, children, women, and powerless men all have to deal with outside authority based on power, so Le Guin has made appropriate choices. Hatfield also suggests that the dragons in Earthsea represent women as Other — a dangerous, powerful, uncontrolled Other. This is very close to Le Guin's own explanation of the dragons in *Earthsea Revisioned*: "The dragon is the stranger, the other, the not-human: a wild spirit, dangerous, winged, which escapes and destroys the artificial order of oppression" (25).

In the 1995 volume of *Children's Literature*, Perry Nodelman, a senior scholar of children's literature, responds to Hatfield's article. In "Reinventing the Past: Gender in Ursula K. Le Guin's *Tehanu* and the Earthsea 'Trilogy,'" Nodelman refutes the notion that the early Earthsea books are implicitly feminist. As Nodelman sees things, Le Guin's perceptions have changed in the intervening years. Because *Tehanu* incorporates Le Guin's changing vision, it challenges readers to question the patriarchal values in the first three books. In actual fact, says Nodelman, as each book was published, it made readers revision the earlier books, so *Tehanu* is simply continuing what Le Guin has been doing with the series all along. Nodelman's conclusion echoes Le Guin's words in *Earthsea Revisioned*: "By showing how much supposedly universal archetypes can change in a decade and a half, *Tehanu* reveals the transitory nature of all the supposedly

eternal assumptions human beings make about gender and sexuality"
(199).

In the science fiction journals, women came to the fore in criticism
about *Tehanu*. In 1995 *Extrapolation* published Holly Littlefield's "Unlearning Patriarchy: Ursula Le Guin's Feminist Consciousness in *The
Tombs of Atuan* and *Tehanu*." Littlefield defends Le Guin as one of the
first writers to experiment with social and gender roles: even her supposedly conventional early science fiction shows a feminine focus on relationships rather than a masculine focus on adventure. Littlefield thinks
Le Guin is explicit in her criticism of patriarchal oppression in *The Tombs
of Atuan*. Though Tenar and other priestesses are isolated from men, men
still control them from outside. Nor is Tenar merely a passive female who
has to be rescued by Ged. As Littlefield notes, "When a fifteen-year-old
girl single-handedly manages to outwit, entrap, and control the most
powerful wizard in the land, it should be obvious that she is not a sim-
pering, helpless female needing some knight in shining armor to rescue
her" (248). This is an intriguing interpretation of Tenar's interaction with
Ged and opens up possibilities for reinterpreting their entire relationship.

In *Tehanu*, Littlefield continues, both Tenar and her author are twenty
years wiser in the ways of the world. Earthsea is bound to look different
through the eyes of Tenar the middle-aged farm wife. Now, instead of
addressing the issue of balance (the Equilibrium), Le Guin is addressing
imbalance in power and gender. Wizards have always been imbalanced
because they exclude women and women's magic completely. But, as Littlefield shows, women's magic has strong ties to dragon magic in Earthsea. Like Len Hatfield, Littlefield sees women linked to dragons in many
ways in this final book. She says that Tenar and her adopted daughter are
both "repeatedly described in dragon terminology" (255).

The abused child Therru is the titular character in *Tehanu*, as the
reader learns at the end of the book. Tehanu is her true name as well as
the name of the guiding star in the heavens. She is also a figure that
should be familiar to Le Guin readers — the maimed child. In a 1997 article in the *New York Review of Science Fiction*, Sandra J. Lindow traces
the figure of the damaged child throughout the Earthsea books, noting
that Ged and Tenar were both abused children. When Tenar rescues
Therru, she is psychologically rescuing the child she herself was. Lindow
notes that age six (Therru's age) seems significant to Le Guin, as her damaged children are often this age. Lindow also links the figure of the
maimed child to Le Guin's account of her illegal abortion in college, published in *Dancing at the Edge of the World* as "The Princess." Lindow explores the damaged child further in *Foundation*'s special issue on
children's literature, showing how the figure recurs in Le Guin's Catwings

books as the abused winged kitten, Jane. In *Earthsea Revisioned*, Le Guin herself sees a connection between Therru and Myra, an injured child in a story finished just before *Tehanu*, "Buffalo Gals, Won't You Come Out Tonight?"

Tracing the image of the maimed child is perhaps the most recent development in Le Guin criticism, but in the wider field of literary criticism, Le Guin has lately become a beacon for everyone who writes about women's literature, particularly in the recent spate of publications on women and utopia or women and science fiction. These are invariably feminist works, but feminism is now sufficiently diffuse to contain contradictory opinions about writers such as Le Guin (writing about men and being a wife and mother no longer disqualify her from the sisterhood). For example, the 1994 collection *Utopian and Science Fiction by Women: Worlds of Difference* contains only one article that specifically discusses Le Guin's works, but the other articles in the collection make constant reference to Le Guin. Similarly, *Frankenstein's Daughters: Women Writing Science Fiction* (1997), by Jane Donawerth (one of the editors of *Utopian and Science Fiction by Women*) contains more references to Le Guin than to any other writer except Joanna Russ. It is no coincidence that Donawerth acclaims both Le Guin and Russ as the foremost feminist critics in science fiction, giving full credit to their early articles in the 1970s for stirring up the winds of change. Donawerth gives them equal billing, even though Russ is a professional academic as well as a science fiction writer and ought therefore to have more critical credibility than the self-proclaimed nonacademic Le Guin.

Even though Le Guin criticism is marching on toward the new millennium, critics have yet to address a large portion of her creative output. Le Guin is the author of five books of poetry — *Wild Angels* (1975), *Hard Words and Other Poems* (1981), *Wild Oats and Fireweed* (1988), *Blue Moon over Thurman Street* (1993), and *Going Out with Peacocks* (1994) — but none of these works has received much critical attention. Only Patrick D. Murphy (author of the incomprehensible ecofeminist sentence quoted in the last chapter) has examined Le Guin's poetry in depth, but his publications are obscure and therefore haven't brought any other criticism to bear. Charlotte Spivack's Twayne volume contains a chapter on the poetry, but it is descriptive rather than explicative.

Le Guin's picture books are also ignored by scholars, although they are reviewed in library journals, children's literature publications, and major newspapers. Her first picture book was *Leese Webster*, published in 1979, which is the story of an artistic spider. She went on to publish *A Visit from Dr. Katz* (1988), *Fire and Stone* (1989), *Fish Soup* (1992), and *A Ride on the Red Mare's Back* (1992). Most of these books were written for

Le Guin's grandchildren. In fairness to children's literature scholars, I must add that picture books in general do not receive much critical attention because they are short, they have few words, and the importance of illustrations requires the critic to be trained in both art and literature. Few picture books are the focus of in-depth scholarly critiques.

Le Guin has also written a series of books for slightly older children about a family of winged cats. *Catwings* (1988), *Catwings Return* (1989), and *Wonderful Alexander and the Catwings* (1994) follow the adventures of four (later five) winged kittens. These books received starred reviews in important children's literature publications, yet the only sustained critical attention they have received is from Sandra Lindow in her 1997 *Foundation* article. From her reader correspondence, Le Guin notes that the Catwings books are particularly meaningful to at-risk children in urban areas, so there may eventually be some scholarly attention from the fields of education and counseling.

Very Far Away from Anywhere Else (1976), Le Guin's one foray into writing realistic fiction for young adults, was another book welcomed by reviewers but shunned by scholars. Even Suzanne Elizabeth Reid's recent Twayne volume on Le Guin as a young adult author devotes a mere one page to a plot summary of this novel, whereas it gives multiple pages to the adult science fiction. No one seems to know what to do with this one contemporary young adult book. One possible reason for the dearth of scholarship may be that the educators most likely to write about this book could be uncomfortable with the fact that both protagonists are brilliant and artistic. Elitism is a kind of unspoken taboo in contemporary young adult literature.

The most recent Le Guin publications also lack serious scholarly scrutiny, but in this case it is too soon to tell whether they will be ignored completely. Generally speaking, there has been a lapse of approximately five years between the appearance of a Le Guin novel and the onset of scholarly attention to it. The only exception is *The Dispossessed*, which benefited from being published on the eve of the special Le Guin issue of *Science-Fiction Studies*. The list of recent books includes Le Guin's two collections of contemporary realistic short stories, *Searoad: Chronicles of Klatsand* (1991) and *Unlocking the Air* (1996); her most recent science fiction stories in *A Fisherman of the Inland Sea* (1994); a collection of four science fiction novellas, *Four Ways to Forgiveness* (1995); and an odd collection of poetry, fantasy, and science fiction called *Buffalo Gals and Other Animal Presences* (1987).

The most egregious scholarly oversight concerns Orsinia, Le Guin's imaginary East European country (named in her own honor), about which she has published both stories — *Orsinian Tales* (1976) — and a novel — *Malafrena* (1979). Before she wrote any fantasy or science fiction, Le Guin had written two novels about Orsinia and two novels set in contemporary America, none of which had found publication. Orsinia is close to her heart, but nobody else expresses much interest in it. The introductory author studies on Le Guin usually mention Orsinia briefly, but the writers of these volumes have little to say. In a 1978 article entitled "Persuading Us to Rejoice and Teaching Us How to Praise: Le Guin's *Orsinian Tales*," James Bittner attempted to pull Orsinia into the critical conversation. Elizabeth Cummins (formerly Cogell) followed his lead in a 1990 article, "The Land-Lady's Homebirth: Revisiting Ursula K. Le Guin's Worlds." In each case, the writer's main interest was connecting Orsinia to Le Guin's other works, much as other science fiction critics had tried to incorporate Earthsea. The interest was not in Orsinia in its own right.

Several of Le Guin's works have received a tiny bit of critical attention. One of these is *The Beginning Place* (1980), a young adult novel that is a peculiar hybrid of realism and fantasy. This novel was reviewed for the *New Yorker* by no less a personage than John Updike, a fact that may explain why it has received some scholarly attention. Updike is complimentary for the most part, but he doesn't like Le Guin's presentation of sex, which he thinks is too simplistic and preachy:

> Read as a metaphor of sexuality emerging from masturbatory solitude into the perilous challenge and exchange of heterosexual encounter, "The Beginning Place" is full of just and subtle touches . . . . This elegant parable of late adolescence fails of credibility only when it presses its moral too earnestly and starts to sound like a marriage manual. (96)

Unlike Flannery O'Connor's *Wise Blood*, Updike writes, *The Beginning Place* does not present a realistic account of the protagonists' first sexual experience. Instead, Le Guin seems to "thump the pulpit" on behalf of the joy of sex (96). Updike's review is longer than most, filling two pages rather than one paragraph. He uses some of that space to provide a quick biography of Le Guin and to connect Le Guin to other authors of science fiction and fantasy. For Updike to devote this much space to a young adult novel is a great compliment to Le Guin.

The annual journal *Children's Literature* published Brian Attebery's interpretation of *The Beginning Place* in 1982. "*The Beginning Place*: Le Guin's Metafantasy" sees the novel as an exploration of the relationship between fantasy and reality in fiction and of the ways fantasy can assist psychological growth. Hugh and Irene, the protagonists, have to defeat a monster in a fantasy world before they can adjust to living in the real world. This beast, which Attebery calls an "undifferentiated essence of

monster" (116) represents the Shadow archetype of each protagonist —
that which is the darkest and worst of him/herself. In the fantasy land
both Hugh and Irene fall in love with people who represent their own
Anima and Animus, but they eventually find real love with each other.

Extrapolation published an article on *The Beginning Place* in 1983, Susan McLean's "*The Beginning Place*: An Interpretation." McLean is interested in incest as a theme in Le Guin's works. Even though the title of her
article indicates a focus on *The Beginning Place*, she first traces incest
through Le Guin's science fiction works. Her survey brings her to the
following conclusion: "The more blatantly Oedipal the love relationship
in Le Guin's works, the more negatively they are presented. In *The Beginning Place*, her most Oedipal book to date, incest is not merely unpleasant
but terrifying" (132). The threat of incest, according to McLean, comes
from Hugh's obsessive mother and Irene's brutal stepfather. Both protagonists project their fear onto the monster. McLean sees the battle with
the monster as "a grotesque parody of sexual intercourse" (137). Hugh
has to kill the monster (fear of sex) before he and Irene are free to make
love. Some of McLean's arguments sound excessive to me; I don't see any
incest in this novel. Since Irene's stepfather is not related to her by blood,
the threat of rape is not really incestuous, and the fact that Hugh's mother
is uncomfortable with his sexuality does not suggest incest to me.

Occasionally one of Le Guin's short stories becomes the focus of critical scrutiny. In 1982 Le Guin published a collection of short stories,
mostly science fiction, called *The Compass Rose*. The three best stories in
this collection are "The New Atlantis," "The Diary of the Rose," and
"Sur." The first two receive occasional mention in articles about Le Guin,
but the final story has drawn individual attention. "Sur" is a delightful and
wryly humorous story about a group of South American women who dis-
cover the South Pole before the famous trips of Amundsen and Scott, but
because they leave nothing behind and don't publish an account of their
adventure, nobody ever knows about them. In a 1986 essay called "Heroes" Le Guin discusses her lifelong fascination with the accounts of dis-
covering the South Pole and credits that fascination with inspiring *The Left
Hand of Darkness*, "in which a Black man from Earth and an androgynous
extraterrestrial pull Scott's sledge through Shackleton's blizzards across a
planet called Winter" (171). Le Guin wanted to accompany the explorers
to the South Pole; since she couldn't, she sent nine South American
women instead. "Sur" is one of Le Guin's favorite stories.

In a 1990 article in *Mythlore*, "Feminist Myth in Le Guin's 'Sur,'"
Barbara Brown examines the story in light of a female heroic that differs
from the traditional male heroic in which manly men conquer nature and
leave physical proof of that fact. In the male heroic, the individual leader

gets all the glory for the expedition. The reader cannot give the glory to the expedition's leader in "Sur," because the narrator, the reluctant nominal leader of the expedition, never gives her own name. She is, in fact, glad that she never has to act as the leader because no emergency ever arises. Unlike the members of the masculine expeditions that preceded them (and failed to reach the pole), the women have no social hierarchies among themselves. The women don't even care if they actually reach the South Pole, whereas that is the entire purpose of the trip for the male expeditions. The women would merely like to see the Pole, if they can do so without undue danger to themselves.

Another difference between the male heroic and the female heroic lies in the way the female expedition deals with the environment. The men built huts and left all kinds of litter behind. The women, on the other hand, live in holes they dig in the ice and they create art out of ice. The women instinctively feel at home in Antarctica instead of feeling they are in a battle with nature. Brown points out that these differences are also reflected in the title of the story, which has many resonances. Besides meaning "south" in Spanish, as a prefix it can mean under or above. The society the women create at the South Pole is a subculture that is above the dominant male culture.

One thing Brown does not notice about the title is that it is also a pun on "sir." This pun is particularly significant in Marleen S. Barr's interpretation of the story. In a book entitled *Lost in Space: Probing Feminist Science Fiction and Beyond*, Barr claims that "Sur," like Le Guin's other works, is both humanist and antihumanist, thus creating an alliance between the liberal and the postmodern:

> Although both patriarchy and the universe do not care whether or not these women reach the South Pole, adhering to humanist rhetoric, they still struggle to do so. In addition, adhering to antihumanist rhetoric, they make no effort to alter the systems of the universe or patriarchy by marking the pole or publishing a report. (158)

Barr's discussion sets up the terms "humanist" and "antihumanist" as another pair of dynamic opposites in Le Guin's works and makes a more sophisticated examination of balanced opposites than did early science fiction critics.

The other stories in *The Compass Rose* have not received this kind of attention, nor have many of Le Guin's other short stories. Now and again an academic critic will refer to one or another of Le Guin's most popular stories while discussing her novels, but on the whole the stories have been ignored in the criticism. Some of them do well in literary anthologies and textbooks, however. "Nine Lives," "The Ones Who Walk Away from

Omelas," "The Day Before the Revolution," and "The New Atlantis" fare particularly well in that regard.

Despite some oversights, Le Guin criticism has come a long way since the 1960s, when Le Guin was fortunate if her work was included in composite reviews in minor science fiction fan magazines. The growth of the criticism has paralleled not only Le Guin's increasing literary stature, but also the development of two new professional fields — children's literature and science fiction. Literary criticism in both of these fields really started in the 1970s, and the criticism has become more and more sophisticated and theoretically informed over the past three decades.

Feminism has been the major critical approach in Le Guin criticism in all three decades, but feminist theory and literary practice have changed considerably during those years. Initial feminist criticism of *The Left Hand of Darkness* gave way to two strands of feminist commentary: the negative remarks continued, but a growing body of feminists began to claim Le Guin as one of their own. Then, after the publication of *Always Coming Home*, there was a backlash of antifeminist criticism. As the feminist criticism grew, it began to incorporate feminist linguistics, utopian criticism, and ecofeminism as well as science fiction. Of all the varieties of feminism, ecofeminism (at least as practiced on Le Guin) boasts the most turgid, incomprehensible, jargon-ridden prose. A bad writing style does not invalidate the ideology, but it presents difficulty in judging the worth of the criticism. Because Le Guin creates entire cultures and environments, her work does lend itself to ecofeminist interpretations, but ecology is not as important to her work as is anthropology. If I had to identify Le Guin with a particular brand of feminism, it would be one that hasn't yet been named. In the 1990s there have been many publications that link feminism, science fiction, and utopian literature as a special study of its own; the writers of such works claim Le Guin as a forerunner. This is not a surprising claim, since Le Guin not only used these philosophies and ideologies in her fiction, but she also wrote essays about them. If this combination of interests ever becomes a genre in its own right, Le Guin will be one of the major figures in it.

Those (if there are any) who doubt that feminism has had an impact on the way we use language need only read through Le Guin criticism from beginning to end. In early reviews the author was referred to in the polite manner of the age either as Miss Le Guin or, if the reviewer knew her marital status, Mrs. Le Guin. Only male writers had the privilege of being referred to by last name only in the 1960s. In the 1970s reviewers and scholars "promoted" Le Guin to the honorific "Ms." Only in the late 1980s did it become commonplace to see the author referred to by last name alone. As critical subject, at least one woman has reached parity with men.

Other than the continuing voice of feminism, scholarship about Le Guin has gone through several critical fads. The earliest criticism looked at two major influences on her work, Taoism and Jungian psychology. Academics mined Le Guin's science fiction and fantasy for every aspect of both. Since the early 1980s, Taoist interpretations have died down. Every now and then, however, there is an odd burp of Taoist criticism. Le Guin's recently published translation of the Tao Te Ching may revive interest. The Jungian criticism, on the other hand, has developed into full-fledged mythological interpretations. Mythological readings began by invoking Northrop Frye, but after a few years scholars moved on to Joseph Campbell. Jung was never far away, because archetypes work very well in Le Guin criticism. By the end of the eighties, though, mythological interpretations of literature had fallen into disfavor and people had turned to other theories.

Anthropological criticism of Le Guin is similar to the mythological. The anthropologists whose names are mentioned in the criticism are usually those who were interested in myth, such as Sir James Frazer and Claude Lévi-Strauss. Rather than being a critical fad, the anthropological interpretations have been a steady drip through the years. Since the heroes of Le Guin's science fiction can easily be seen as cultural anthropologists, they are often the focus of such articles, but all of Le Guin's books have a share in this criticism because she invariably builds entire cultures in her works.

Another common concern of the criticism has been theme and/or images in Le Guin's works. Critics are prone to label almost anything a theme, so sometimes Taoism is a theme rather than an influence. Sometimes anthropology or feminism is a theme. Critics have also found the following themes in Le Guin's works: communication, sex, science, touch, forests, death, balanced opposites, religion, creativity, anarchy, ecology, telepathy, power, and so on. Images are a bit easier to recognize; for example, critics have noted in individual works a use of web imagery. One critic will mention spider images in Earthsea; another will see them in *Always Coming Home*. But no one has put it all together yet. Images of winter landscapes or forests are especially noticeable in Le Guin's early work. Wall imagery stands out in *The Dispossessed*, and the hinge is primary in *Always Coming Home*. Light and dark imagery is endemic, as indeed are all forms of imagery that lend themselves to a yin/yang arrangement. Critics have continued to examine this aspect of Le Guin's work throughout the years.

Other people have examined the structure of Le Guin's novels. This kind of criticism started in the 1970s with articles about specific texts. Because *The Left Hand of Darkness, The Dispossessed,* and *Always Coming Home* have unusual structures, they are the focus of many of these articles. Lately, however, such commentary has faded, perhaps because Le Guin does not seem to be employing such experimental structures in her latest books. She has returned to more traditional chronological narratives lately, but only because those forms suit the stories she wants to tell. She continues to invent new story structures as she needs them.

Finally, there are critics who look at Le Guin's use of language. Sometimes these critics apply communication theories and sometimes they apply linguistic theories. There are only a handful of such articles, and they don't form a coherent whole. Lately the linguistic approach has been subsumed by feminist criticism concerned with recovering a monther tongue.

Le Guin has been an interested observer/participant in most of the critical approaches — an ideal role for a person raised by anthropologists. She has listened to the dragons speak, and she has responded in their own language. Even that has changed, however. In her maturity Le Guin is very like the adult Tenar in her outlook. This description of Tenar among the king's men could be a description of Le Guin's attitude to the critics:

> We are so polite, she thought, all Ladies and Lords and Masters, all bows and compliments . . . . She felt as she had felt in Havnor as a girl: a barbarian, uncouth among their smoothnesses. But because she was not a girl now, she was not awed, but only wondered at how men ordered their world into this dance of masks, and how easily a woman might learn to dance it. (*Tehanu* 137–38)

In her early years as a writer, Le Guin tried to learn this critical dance. The dragons were willing to speak with her rather than eat her. As a mature woman, however, she chooses when and where and whether she wishes to speak to them, and she chooses to speak in her own language rather than in theirs. She is dancing her own dance now; if the dragons want to join in, they may.

Works Cited

Attebery, Brian. "*The Beginning Place*: Le Guin's Metafantasy." *Children's Literature* 10 (1982): 113–23.

Barr, Marleen S. *Lost in Space: Probing Feminist Science Fiction and Beyond.* Chapel Hill: The U of North Carolina P, 1993.

Bittner, James W. "Persuading Us to Rejoice and Teaching Us How to Praise: Le Guin's *Orsinian Tales*." *Science-Fiction Studies* 5 (November 1978): 215–42.

Brown, Barbara. "Feminist Myth in Le Guin's 'Sur.'" *Mythlore* 16 (Summer 1990): 56–59.

Clute, John. "Deconstructing Paradise." Rev. of *Tehanu: The Last Book of Earthsea*. *Times Literary Supplement* 28 December 1990: 1409.

Cummins, Elizabeth. "The Land-Lady's Homebirth: Revisiting Ursula K. Le Guin's Worlds." *Science-Fiction Studies* 17 (July 1990): 153–66.

Dirda, Michael. "The Twilight of an Age of Magic." Rev. of *Tehanu: The Last Book of Earthsea*. *Washington Post* (Book World) 25 February 1990: 1.

Disch, Thomas M. "Big Ideas and Dead-End Thrills." *Atlantic* 269 (February 1992): 86–94.

Donawerth, Jane. *Frankenstein's Daughters: Women Writing Science Fiction*. Syracuse: Syracuse UP, 1997.

Donawerth, Jane, and Carol A. Kolmerten, eds. *Utopian and Science Fiction by Women: Worlds of Difference*. Syracuse: Syracuse UP, 1994.

Hatfield, Len. "From Master to Brother: Shifting the Balance of Authority in Ursula K. Le Guin's *Farthest Shore* and *Tehanu*." *Children's Literature* 21 (1993): 43–65.

Le Guin, Ursula K. *Always Coming Home*. New York: Harper & Row, 1985.

——. *The Beginning Place*. New York: Harper & Row, 1980.

——. *Blue Moon over Thurman Street*. Portland: New Sage Press, 1993.

——. *Buffalo Gals and Other Animal Presences*. Santa Barbara: Capra Press, 1987.

——. "The Carrier Bag Theory of Fiction." *Dancing at the Edge of the World: Thoughts on Words, Women, Places*. New York: Grove Press, 1989. New York: Harper & Row/Perennial Library, 1990. 165–70.

——. *Catwings*. New York: Orchard Books, 1988.

——. *Catwings Return*. New York: Orchard Books, 1989.

——. *The Compass Rose*. New York: Harper & Row, 1982.

——. *Earthsea Revisioned*. Cambridge: Green Bay Publications, 1993.

——. *Fire and Stone*. New York: Atheneum, 1989.

——. *Fish Soup*. New York: Atheneum, 1992.

——. *A Fisherman of the Inland Sea*. New York: HarperPrism, 1994.

——. *Four Ways to Forgiveness*. New York: HarperPrism, 1995.

——. *Going Out with Peacocks and Other Poems*. New York: HarperPerennial, 1994.

——. *Hard Words and Other Poems*. New York: Harper & Row, 1981.

——. "Heroes." *Dancing at the Edge of the World: Thoughts on Words, Women, Places*. New York: Grove Press, 1989. New York: Harper & Row/Perennial Library, 1990. 171–75.

——. *Lao Tzu: Tao Te Ching*. Boston: Shambhala Publications, 1997.

——. *Leese Webster*. New York: Atheneum, 1979.

——. *Malafrena*. New York: Putnam's, 1979.

——. *Orsinian Tales*. New York: Harper & Row, 1976.

——. "The Princess." *Dancing at the Edge of the World: Thoughts on Words, Women, Places*. New York: Grove Press, 1989. New York: Harper & Row/Perennial Library, 1990. 75–79.

——. *A Ride on the Red Mare's Back*. New York: Orchard Books, 1992.

——. *Searoad: Chronicles of Klatsand*. New York: HarperCollins, 1991.

——. *Tehanu: The Last Book of Earthsea*. New York: Atheneum, 1990.

——. *Unlocking the Air and Other Stories*. New York: HarperCollins, 1996.

——. *Very Far Away from Anywhere Else*. New York: Atheneum, 1976.

——. *A Visit from Dr. Katz*. New York: Atheneum, 1988.

——. *Wild Angels*. Santa Barbara: Capra Press, 1975.

——. *Wild Oats and Fireweed: New Poems*. New York: Perennial Library, 1988.

——. *Wonderful Alexander and the Catwings*. New York: Orchard Books, 1994.

Lindow, Sandra. "Trauma and Recovery in Ursula K. Le Guin's *Wonderful Alexander*. Animal as Guide Through the Inner Space of the Unconscious." *Foundation* 70 (Summer 1997): 32–38.

——. "Ursula K. Le Guin's Earthsea: Rescuing the Damaged Child." *New York Review of Science Fiction* 9.5 (January 1997): 1, 10–13.

Littlefield, Holly. "Unlearning Patriarchy: Ursula Le Guin's Feminist Consciousness in *The Tombs of Atuan* and *Tehanu*." *Extrapolation* 16 (Fall 1995): 244–58.

McKinley, Robin. "The Woman Wizard's Triumph." Rev. of *Tehanu: The Last Book of Earthsea*. *New York Times Book Review* 20 May 1990: 38.

McLean, Susan. "*The Beginning Place*: An Interpretation." *Extrapolation* 24 (Summer 1983): 130–42.

Nodelman, Perry. "Reinventing the Past: Gender in Ursula K. Le Guin's *Tehanu* and the Earthsea 'Trilogy.'" *Children's Literature* 23 (1995): 179–201.

Reid, Suzanne Elizabeth. *Presenting Ursula K. Le Guin*. Twayne's United States Authors Series 677. New York: Twayne Publishers, 1997.

Spivack, Charlotte. *Ursula K. Le Guin*. Twayne's United States Author Series 453. Boston: Twayne, 1984.

Updike, John. "Imaginary Things." Rev. of *The Beginning Place*. *New Yorker* 23 June 1980: 94, 96–97.

Primary Bibliography

Works by Ursula K. Le Guin

"April in Paris." *Fantastic* 11 (September 1962): 54–65.

"The Masters." *Fantastic* 12 (February 1963): 85–99.

"Darkness Box." *Fantastic* 12 (November 1963): 60–67.

"The Word of Unbinding." *Fantastic* 13 (January 1964): 67–73.

"The Rule of Names." *Fantastic* 13 (April 1964): 79–88.

"Selection." *Amazing* 38 (August 1964): 36–45.

"The Dowry of Angyar." *Amazing* 38 (September 1964): 46–63.

Rocannon's World. New York: Ace, 1966.

Planet of Exile. New York: Ace, 1966.

City of Illusions. New York: Ace, 1967.

A Wizard of Earthsea. Berkeley: Parnassus Press, 1968.

The Left Hand of Darkness. New York: Ace, 1969.

"Nine Lives." *Playboy* 16 (November 1969): 128–29, 132, 220–30.

"A Trip to the Head." *Quark 1.* Ed. Samuel R. Delany and Marilyn Hacker. New York: Paperback Library, 1970. 36–42.

The Tombs of Atuan. New York: Atheneum, 1971.

The Lathe of Heaven. New York: Scribner's, 1971.

"Vaster Than Empires and More Slow." *New Dimensions I.* Ed. Robert Silverberg. Garden City: Doubleday, 1971. 87–121.

"The Word for World Is Forest." *Again, Dangerous Visions.* Ed. Harlan Ellison. Garden City: Doubleday, 1972. 30–108.

The Farthest Shore. New York: Atheneum, 1972.

"The Ones Who Walk Away from Omelas." *New Dimensions III.* Ed. Robert Silverberg. New York: Signet, 1973. 1–7.

The Dispossessed: An Ambiguous Utopia. New York: Harper & Row, 1974.

"The Day Before the Revolution." *Galaxy* 35 (August 1974): 17–30.

"The New Atlantis." *The New Atlantis and Other Novellas of Science Fiction.* Ed. Robert Silverberg. New York: Hawthorn, 1975. 57–86.

The Wind's Twelve Quarters. New York: Harper & Row, 1975.

Wild Angels. Santa Barbara: Capra Press, 1975.

Orsinian Tales. New York: Harper & Row, 1976.

Very Far Away from Anywhere Else. New York: Atheneum, 1976.

"The Eye of the Heron." *Millennial Women.* Ed. Virginia Kidd. New York: Delacorte, 1978. 124–302.

Leese Webster. New York: Atheneum, 1979.

Malafrena. New York: Putnam's, 1979.

The Beginning Place. New York: Harper & Row, 1980.

Hard Words and Other Poems. New York: Harper & Row, 1981.

The Compass Rose. New York: Harper & Row, 1982.

Always Coming Home. New York: Harper & Row, 1985.

Buffalo Gals and Other Animal Presences. Santa Barbara: Capra Press, 1987.

Wild Oats and Fireweed: New Poems. New York: Perennial Library, 1988.

A Visit from Dr. Katz. New York: Atheneum, 1988.

Catwings. New York: Orchard Books, 1988.

Catwings Return. New York: Orchard Books, 1989.

Fire and Stone. New York: Atheneum, 1989.

Tehanu: The Last Book of Earthsea. New York: Atheneum, 1990.

Searoad: Chronicles of Klatsand. New York: HarperCollins, 1991.

Fish Soup. New York: Atheneum, 1992.

A Ride on the Red Mare's Back. New York: Orchard Books, 1992.

Blue Moon over Thurman Street. Portland: New Sage Press, 1993.

Wonderful Alexander and the Catwings. New York: Orchard Books, 1994.

A Fisherman of the Inland Sea. New York: HarperPrism, 1994.

Going Out with Peacocks and Other Poems. New York: HarperPerennial, 1994.

Four Ways to Forgiveness. New York: HarperPrism, 1995.

Unlocking the Air and Other Stories. New York: HarperCollins, 1996.

Fiction Works by Other Writers

Kroeber, Theodora. *Ishi, Last of His Tribe.* Berkeley: Parnassus Press, 1964.

Alexander, Lloyd. *The Book of Three.* New York: Holt, 1964.

———. *The Black Cauldron.* New York: Holt, 1965.

Tolkien, J. R. R. *The Lord of the Rings.* New York: Ballantine, 1965.

Alexander, Lloyd. *The Castle of Llyr.* New York: Holt, 1966.

Davidson, Avram. *The Kar-Chee Reign.* New York: Ace, 1966.

Disch, Thomas M. *Mankind Under the Leash.* New York: Ace, 1966.

Hinton, S. E. *The Outsiders.* New York: Viking, 1967.

Hamilton, Virginia. *The Planet of Junior Brown.* New York: Macmillan, 1971.

O'Brien, Robert C. *Mrs. Frisby and the Rats of NIMH.* New York: Macmillan, 1971.

Works Cited[1]

Works by Le Guin

Letter to the editor. *SF Commentary* 26 (April 1971): 90–93.

From Elfland to Poughkeepsie. Portland: Pendragon Press, 1973.

"Dreams Must Explain Themselves." *Algol* 21 (November 1973): 7–10, 12, 14.

"Why Are Americans Afraid of Dragons?" *Pacific Northwest Library Association Quarterly* 38 (Winter 1974): 14–18.

"The Child and the Shadow." *Quarterly Journal of The Library of Congress* 32 (April 1975): 139–48.

"Ketterer on *The Left Hand of Darkness.*" *Science-Fiction Studies* 2 (July 1975): 137–39.

"Is Gender Necessary?" *Aurora: Beyond Equality.* Ed. Vonda N. McIntyre and Susan Janice Anderson. Greenwich, CT: Fawcett, 1976. 130–39.

The Language of the Night: Essays on Fantasy and Science Fiction. Ed. Susan Wood. New York: G. P. Putnam's, 1979.

Letter to the editor. *Isaac Asimov's Science Fiction Magazine* (April 1987): 14.

Dancing at the Edge of the World: Thoughts on Words, Women, Places. New York: Grove Press, 1989.

---

[1]   Please note that Works Cited is in chronological order so as to document the reception of U. K. Le Guin's works. The reader can locate works cited by author in the index.

"Is Gender Necessary? Redux." *The Language of the Night*. Rev. ed. London: Women's Press, 1989. 155–72.

Earthsea Revisioned. Cambridge: Green Bay Publications, 1993.

Lao Tzu: Tao Te Ching. Translated by Le Guin. Boston: Shambhala Publications, 1997.

Works by Others

Campbell, Joseph. *The Hero with a Thousand Faces*. Princeton: Princeton UP, 1953.

Frye, Northrop. *Anatomy of Criticism*. Princeton: Princeton UP, 1957.

Cawthorn, James. "I Love You, Semantics." Rev. of *Rocannon's World*. *New Worlds* 49 (August 1966): 147.

Merril, Judith. Rev. of *Rocannon's World*. *Fantasy and Science Fiction* 31 (December 1966): 33.

Bangsund, John. Rev. of *City of Illusions*. *Australian Science Fiction Review* 10 (June 1967): 65–66.

Miller, P. Schuyler. Rev. of *Rocannon's World*. *Analog* 80 (November 1967): 166.

Hinton, S. E. "Teen-Agers Are for Real." *New York Times Book Review* 27 August 1967: 26–29.

Viguers, Ruth H. Rev. of *A Wizard of Earthsea*. *Horn Book* 45 (February 1969): 59–60.

Harmon, Elva. Rev. of *A Wizard of Earthsea*. *Library Journal* 94 (15 May 1969): 2104.

Panshin, Alexei. "Books." Rev. of *The Left Hand of Darkness*. *Fantasy and Science Fiction* 37 (November 1969): 50–51.

Suvin, Darko. "The SF Novel in 1969." *Nebula Award Stories 5*. Ed. James Blish. London: Gollancz, 1970. 193–205.

Cameron, Eleanor. "High Fantasy: *A Wizard of Earthsea*." *Horn Book* 47 (April 1971): 129–38.

Lewis, Naomi. "The Making of a Mage." Rev. of *A Wizard of Earthsea*. *Times Literary Supplement* 2 April 1971: 383.

Lem, Stanislaw. "Lost Opportunities." *SF Commentary* 24 (November 1971): 22–24.

White, Ted. Rev. of *The Tombs of Atuan*. *Fantastic Science Fiction* 2 (February 1972): 112–13.

Smith, Jennifer Farley. "Despair Pervades Prize Books." *Christian Science Monitor* 2 May 1972: 4.

Sturgeon, Theodore. Rev. of *The Lathe of Heaven*. *New York Times Book Review* 14 May 1972: 33.

Townsend, John Rowe. "Four Myths and Only One Hit." Rev. of *The Tombs of Atuan. Guardian* (London) 17 May 1972: 9.

"Myths of Anti-Climax." Rev. of *The Lathe of Heaven. Times Literary Supplement* 23 June 1972: 705.

Jago, Wendy. "'A Wizard of Earthsea' and the Charge of Escapism." *Children's Literature in Education* 8 (July 1972): 21–29.

Russ, Joanna. "The Image of Women in Science Fiction." *Images of Women in Fiction: Feminist Perspectives*. Ed. Susan Koppelman Cornillon. Bowling Green: Bowling Green U Popular P, 1972. 79–94.

Friend, Beverly. "Virgin Territory: Women and Sex in Science Fiction." *Extrapolation* 14 (December 1972): 49–58.

Fox, Geoff, ed. "Notes on 'Teaching' *A Wizard of Earthsea*." *Children's Literature in Education* 11 (May 1973): 58–67.

Nicholls, Peter. "Showing Children the Value of Death." Rev. of *The Farthest Shore. Foundation* 5 (January 1974): 71–80.

Barbour, Douglas. "*The Lathe of Heaven*: Taoist Dream." *Algol* 21 (November 1973): 22–24.

Scholes, Robert. "The Good Witch of the West." *Hollins Critic* 11 (April 1974): 1–12.

Barbour, Douglas. "On Ursula Le Guin's *A Wizard of Earthsea*." *Riverside Quarterly* 6 (April 1974): 119–23.

Barbour, Douglas. "Wholeness and Balance in the Hainish Novels of Ursula K. Le Guin." *Science-Fiction Studies* 1 (Spring 1974): 164–73.

Ketterer, David. *New Worlds for Old: The Apocalyptic Imagination, Science Fiction, and American Literature*. Bloomington: Indiana UP, 1974.

Hamilton-Paterson, James. "Allegorical Imperatives." Rev. of *The Dispossessed. Times Literary Supplement* 20 June 1975: 704.

Ketterer, David. "In Response." *Science-Fiction Studies* 2 (July 1975): 139–46.

Suvin, Darko. "Introductory Note: The Science Fiction of Ursula K. Le Guin." *Science-Fiction Studies* 2 (November 1975): 203–4.

Nudelman, Rafail. "An Approach to the Structure of Le Guin's SF." *Science-Fiction Studies* 2 (November 1975): 210–20.

Jameson, Fredric. "World-Reduction in Le Guin: The Emergence of Utopian Narrative." *Science-Fiction Studies* 2 (November 1975): 221–30.

Watson, Ian. "The Forest as Metaphor for Mind: 'The Word for World Is Forest' and 'Vaster Than Empires and More Slow.'" *Science-Fiction Studies* 2 (November 1975): 231–37.

Huntington, John. "Public and Private Imperatives in Le Guin's Novels." *Science-Fiction Studies* 2 (November 1975): 237–43.

Porter, David L. "The Politics of Le Guin's Opus." *Science-Fiction Studies* 2 (November 1975): 243–48.

Bierman, Judah. "Ambiguity in Utopia: *The Dispossessed.*" *Science-Fiction Studies* 2 (November 1975): 249–55.

Theall, Donald F. "The Art of Social-Science Fiction: The Ambiguous Utopian Dialects of Ursula K. Le Guin." *Science-Fiction Studies* 2 (November 1975): 256–64.

Suvin, Darko. "Parables of De-Alienation: Le Guin's Widdershins Dance." *Science-Fiction Studies* 2 (November 1975): 265–74.

Rappaport, Karen. Rev. of *The Farthest Shore. Science Fiction Review Monthly* 9 (November 1975): 15.

Scholes, Robert. *Structural Fabulation: An Essay on Fiction of the Future.* Notre Dame: U of Notre Dame P, 1975.

Elliott, Robert C. "A New Utopian Novel." Rev. of *The Dispossessed. Yale Review* 65 (Winter 1976): 256–61.

Slusser, George Edgar. *The Farthest Shores of Ursula K. Le Guin.* Popular Writers of Today 3. San Bernardino: The Borgo Press, 1976.

Barbour, Douglas. "Patterns and Meaning in the Novels of Ursula K. Le Guin, Joanna Russ and Samuel R. Delany, 1962–1972." Ph.D. dissertation, Queen's University (Canada), 1976.

Bickman, Martin. "Le Guin's *The Left Hand of Darkness*: Form and Content." *Science-Fiction Studies* 4 (March 1977): 42–47.

Delany, Samuel R. "To Read *The Dispossessed.*" *The Jewel-Hinged Jaw: Notes on the Language of Science Fiction.* Elizabethtown, NY: Dragon Press, 1977. 239–308.

Esmonde, Margaret P. "The Gift of Men: Death and Deathlessness in Children's Fantasy." *Fantasiae* 7.9 (April 1979): 1, 8–11.

Shippey, T. A. "The Magic Art and the Evolution of Words: Ursula Le Guin's Earthsea Trilogy." *Mosaic* 10 (Winter 1977): 147–63.

Williams, Raymond. "Utopia and Science Fiction." *Science-Fiction Studies* 5 (November 1978): 203–14.

Bittner, James W. "Persuading Us to Rejoice and Teaching Us How to Praise: Le Guin's *Orsinian Tales.*" *Science-Fiction Studies* 5 (November 1978): 215–42.

Walker, Jeanne Murray. "Myth, Exchange and History in *The Left Hand of Darkness. Science-Fiction Studies* 6 (July 1979): 180–89.

White, Virginia L. "Bright the Hawk's Flight: The Journey of the Hero in Ursula Le Guin's Earthsea Trilogy." *Forum* 20 (1979): 34–45.

Esmonde, Margaret P. "The Master Pattern: The Psychological Journey in the Earthsea Trilogy." *Ursula K. Le Guin.* Ed. Joseph D. Olander and Martin Harry Greenberg. Writers of the 21st Century Series. New York: Taplinger, 1979. 15–35.

Smith, Philip E., II. "Unbuilding Walls: Human Nature and the Nature of Evolutionary and Political Theory in *The Dispossessed.*" *Ursula K. Le Guin.* Ed. Joseph D. Olander and Martin Harry Greenberg. Writers of the 21st Century Series. New York: Taplinger, 1979. 77–96.

Hayles, N. B. "Androgyny, Ambivalence, and Assimilation in *The Left Hand of Darkness.*" *Ursula K. Le Guin.* Ed. Joseph D. Olander and Martin Harry Greenberg. Writers of the 21st Century Series. New York: Taplinger, 1979. 97–115.

Brennan, John P., and Michael C. Downs. "Anarchism and Utopian Tradition in *The Dispossessed. Ursula K. Le Guin.* Ed. Joseph D. Olander and Martin Harry Greenberg. Writers of the 21st Century Series. New York: Taplinger, 1979. 116–52.

Remington, Thomas J. "The Other Side of Suffering: Touch as Theme and Metaphor in Le Guin's Science Fiction Novels." *Ursula K. Le Guin.* Ed. Joseph D. Olander and Martin Harry Greenberg. Writers of the 21st Century Series. New York: Taplinger, 1979. 153–77.

Gunew, Sneja. "Mythic Reversals: The Evolution of the Shadow Motif." *Ursula K. Le Guin.* Ed. Joseph D. Olander and Martin Harry Greenberg. Writers of the 21st Century Series. New York: Taplinger, 1979. 178–99.

Crow, John H., and Richard D. Erlich. "Words of Binding: Patterns of Integration in the Earthsea Trilogy." *Ursula K. Le Guin.* Ed. Joseph D. Olander and Martin Harry Greenberg. Writers of the 21st Century Series. New York: Taplinger, 1979. 200–224.

Bittner, James W. "A Survey of Le Guin Criticism." *Ursula K. Le Guin: Voyager to Inner Lands and to Outer Space.* Ed. Joe De Bolt. Literary Criticism Series. Port Washington, NY: Kennikat Press, 1979. 31–49.

Sinclair, Karen. "Solitary Being: The Hero as Anthropologist." *Ursula K. Le Guin: Voyager to Inner Lands and to Outer Space.* Ed. Joe De Bolt. Literary Criticism Series. Port Washington, NY: Kennikat Press, 1979. 50–65.

Koper, Peter T. "Science and Rhetoric in the Fiction of Ursula Le Guin." *Ursula K. Le Guin: Voyager to Inner Lands and to Outer Space.* Ed. Joe De Bolt. Literary Criticism Series. Port Washington, NY: Kennikat Press, 1979. 66–86.

Lasseter, Rollin A. "Four Letters about Le Guin." *Ursula K. Le Guin: Voyager to Inner Lands and to Outer Space.* Ed. Joe De Bolt. Literary Criticism Series. Port Washington, NY: Kennikat Press, 1979. 89–114.

Pfeiffer, John R. "'But Dragons Have Keen Ears': On Hearing 'Earthsea' with Recollections of 'Beowulf.'" *Ursula K. Le Guin: Voyager to Inner Lands and to Outer Space.* Ed. Joe De Bolt. Literary Criticism Series. Port Washington, NY: Kennikat Press, 1979. 115–27.

Molson, Francis J. "The Earthsea Trilogy: Ethical Fantasy for Children." *Ursula K. Le Guin: Voyager to Inner Lands and to Outer Space.* Ed. Joe De Bolt. Literary Criticism Series. Port Washington, NY: Kennikat Press, 1979. 128–49.

Cogell, Elizabeth Cummins. "Taoist Configurations: 'The Dispossessed.'" *Ursula K. Le Guin: Voyager to Inner Lands and to Outer Space.* Ed. Joe De Bolt. Literary Criticism Series. Port Washington, NY: Kennikat Press, 1979. 153–79.

Tifft, Larry L., and Dennis C. Sullivan. "Possessed Sociology and Le Guin's *Dispossessed*: From Exile to Anarchism." *Ursula K. Le Guin: Voyager to Inner Lands and to Outer Space.* Ed. Joe De Bolt. Literary Criticism Series. Port Washington, NY: Kennikat Press, 1979. 180–97.

Walker, Jeanne Murray. "Rites of Passage Today: The Cultural Significance of *A Wizard of Earthsea*." *Mosaic* 13 (Spring/Summer 1980): 179–91.

Updike, John. "Imaginary Things." Rev. of *The Beginning Place*. *New Yorker* 23 June 1980: 94, 96–97.

Moylan, Tom. "Beyond Negation: The Critical Utopias of Ursula K. Le Guin and Samuel R. Delany." *Extrapolation* 21 (Fall 1980): 236–53.

Bailey, Edgar C., Jr. "Shadows in Earthsea: Le Guin's Use of a Jungian Archetype." *Extrapolation* 21 (Fall 1980): 254–61.

Remington, Thomas J. "A Time to Live and a Time to Die: Cyclical Renewal in the Earthsea Trilogy." *Extrapolation* 21 (Fall 1980): 278–86.

Manlove, C. N. "Conservatism in the Fantasy of Le Guin." *Extrapolation* 21 (Fall 1980): 287–97.

Spencer, Kathleen. "Exiles and Envoys: The SF of Ursula K. Le Guin." *Foundation* 20 (October 1980): 32–43.

Attebery, Brian. *The Fantasy Tradition in American Literature: From Irving to Le Guin.* Bloomington: Indiana UP, 1980.

Rees, David. *The Marble in the Water: Essays on Contemporary Writers of Fiction for Children and Young Adults.* Boston: Horn Book, 1980.

Braswell, Laurel. "The Visionary Voyage in Science Fiction and Medieval Allegory." *Mosaic* 14 (Winter 1981): 125–42.

Esmonde, Margaret P. "The Good Witch of the West." *Children's Literature* 9 (1981): 185–90.

Farrelly, James P. "The Promised Land: Moses, Nearing, Skinner, and Le Guin." *JGE: The Journal of General Education* 33 (Spring 1981): 15–23.

Lake, David J. "Le Guin's Twofold Vision: Contrary Image-Sets in *The Left Hand of Darkness.*" *Science-Fiction Studies* 8 (July 1981): 156–64.

Bucknall, Barbara J. *Ursula K. Le Guin.* New York: Frederick Ungar, 1981.

Algeo, John. "Magic Names: Onomastics in the Fantasies of Ursula Le Guin." *Names* 30.2 (1982): 59–67.

Attebery, Brian. "*The Beginning Place*: Le Guin's Metafantasy." *Children's Literature* 10 (1982): 113–23.

Cogell, Wayne. "The Absurdity of Sartre's Ontology: A Response by Ursula K. Le Guin." *Philosophers Look at Science Fiction.* Ed. Nicholas D. Smith. Chicago: Nelson-Hall, 1982. 143–51.

Myers, Doris T. "'True Speech' in the Fantasies of Tolkien and Le Guin." *Forum Linguisticum* 7.2 (December 1982): 95–106.

Cogell, Elizabeth Cummins. *Ursula K. Le Guin: A Primary and Secondary Bibliography.* Boston: G. K. Hall, 1983.

McLean, Susan. "*The Beginning Place*: An Interpretation." *Extrapolation* 24 (Summer 1983): 130–42.

Myers, Victoria. "Conversational Techniques in Ursula Le Guin: A Speech-Act Analysis." *Science-Fiction Studies* 10 (November 1983): 306–16.

Bittner, James W. "Chronosophy, Aesthetics, and Ethics in Le Guin's *The Dispossessed: An Ambiguous Utopia.*" *No Place Else: Explorations in Utopian and Dystopian Fiction.* Ed. Eric S. Rabkin, Martin H. Greenberg, and Joseph D. Olander. Carbondale: Southern Illinois UP, 1983. 244–70.

Somay, Bulent. "Towards an Open-Ended Utopia." *Science-Fiction Studies* 11 (March 1984): 25–38.

Spivack, Charlotte. "'Only in dying life': the Dynamics of Old Age in the Fiction of Ursula Le Guin." *Modern Language Studies* 14 (Summer 1984): 43–53.

Spivack, Charlotte. *Ursula K. Le Guin.* Twayne's United States Authors Series 453. Boston: Twayne, 1984.

Bittner, James W. *Approaches to the Fiction of Ursula K. Le Guin.* Studies in Speculative Fiction No. 4. Ann Arbor: UMI Research Press, 1984.

Kuznets, Lois R. "'High Fantasy' in America: A Study of Lloyd Alexander, Ursula Le Guin, and Susan Cooper." *The Lion and the Unicorn* 9 (1985): 19–35.

Delany, Samuel R. Rev. of *Always Coming Home. New York Times Book Review* 29 September 1985: 31–32.

Aldiss, Brian. Rev. of *Always Coming Home. Washington Post* (Book World) 6 October 1985: 11.

Prescott, Peter S. Rev. of *Always Coming Home. Newsweek* 18 November 1985: 101.

Burton, Deirdre. "Linguistic Innovation in Feminist Utopian Fiction." *Ilha-do-Desterro: A Journal of Language and Literature* 14.2 (1985): 82–106.

Bloom, Harold, ed. *Ursula K. Le Guin.* Modern Critical Views. New York: Chelsea House, 1986.

Lamb, Patricia Frazer, and Diana L. Veith. "Again, *The Left Hand of Darkness:* Androgyny or Homophobia?" *Erotic Universe: Sexuality and Fantastic Literature.* Ed. Donald Palumbo. Contributions to the Study of Science Fiction and Fantasy No. 18. Westport, CT: Greenwood Press, 1986. 221–31.

Wytenbroek, J. R. "*Always Coming Home:* Pacificism [*sic*] and Anarchy in Le Guin's Utopia." *Extrapolation* 28 (Winter 1987): 330–39.

Sherman, Cordelia. "The Princess and the Wizard: The Fantasy Worlds of Ursula K. Le Guin and George MacDonald." *Children's Literature Association Quarterly* 12 (Spring 1987): 24–28.

Erlich, Richard D. "Ursula K. Le Guin and Arthur C. Clarke on Immanence, Transcendence, and Massacres." *Extrapolation* 28 (Summer 1987): 105–29.

Bloom, Harold, ed. *Ursula K. Le Guin's The Left Hand of Darkness.* Modern Critical Interpretations. New York: Chelsea House, 1987.

Esmonde, Margaret P. "Beyond the Circles of the World: Death and the Hereafter in Children's Literature." *Webs and Wardrobes: Humanist and Religious World Views in Children's Literature.* Ed. Joseph O'Beirne and Lucy Floyd Morcock Milner. Lanham, MD: UP of America, 1987. 34–45.

Benford, Gregory. "Reactionary Utopias." *Storm Warnings: Science Fiction Confronts the Future.* Ed. George E. Slusser, Colin Greenland, and Eric S. Rabkin. Carbondale: Southern Illinois UP, 1987. 73–83.

Shippey, T. A. "Variations on Newspeak: The Open Question of *Nineteen Eighty-Four.*" *Storm Warnings: Science Fiction Confronts the Future.* Ed. George E. Slusser, Colin Greenland, and Eric S. Rabkin. Carbondale: Southern Illinois UP, 1987. 172–93.

Tavormina, M. Teresa. "A Gate of Horn and Ivory: Dreaming True and False in Earthsea." *Extrapolation* 29 (Winter 1988): 338–48.

Murphy, Patrick D. "Robinson Jeffers's Influence on Ursula K. Le Guin." *Robinson Jeffers Newsletter* 72 (March 1988): 20–22.

Jacobs, Naomi. "Beyond Stasis and Symmetry: Lessing, Le Guin, and the Remodeling of Utopia." *Extrapolation* 29 (Spring 1988): 34–45.

Selinger, Bernard. *Le Guin and Identity in Contemporary Fiction.* Studies in Speculative Fiction No. 16. Ann Arbor: UMI Research Press, 1988.

Hovanec, Carol P. "Visions of Nature in *The Word for World is Forest:* A Mirror of the American Consciousness." *Extrapolation* 30 (Spring 1989): 84–91.

Stone-Blackburn, Susan. "Adult Telepathy: *Babel-17* and *The Left Hand of Darkness.*" *Extrapolation* 30 (Fall 1989): 243–53.

Murphy, Patrick D. "The Left Hand of Fabulation: The Poetry of Ursula K. Le Guin." *The Poetic Fantastic: Studies in an Evolving Genre*. Ed. Patrick D. Murphy and Vernon Hyles. Contributions to the Study of Science Fiction and Fantasy 40. Westport, CT: Greenwood Press, 1989. 123–36.

Dirda, Michael. "The Twilight of an Age of Magic." Rev. of *Tehanu*. *Washington Post* (Book World) 25 February 1990: 1.

Brown, Barbara. "Feminist Myth in Le Guin's 'Sur.'" *Mythlore* 16 (Summer 1990): 56–59.

Cummins, Elizabeth. "The Land-Lady's Homebirth: Revisiting Ursula K. Le Guin's Worlds." *Science-Fiction Studies* 17 (July 1990): 153–66.

Cummins, Elizabeth. *Understanding Ursula K. Le Guin*. Columbia, SC: U of South Carolina P, 1990.

Khanna, Lee Cullen. "Women's Utopias: New Worlds, New Texts." *Feminism, Utopia, and Narrative*. Ed. Libby Falk Jones and Sarah Webster Goodwin. Tennessee Studies in Literature 32. Knoxville: U of Tennessee P, 1990. 130–40.

Fitting, Peter. "The Turn from Utopia in Recent Feminist Fiction." *Feminism, Utopia, and Narrative*. Ed. Libby Falk Jones and Sarah Webster Goodwin. Tennessee Studies in Literature 32. Knoxville: U of Tennessee P, 1990. 141–58.

Clute, John. "Deconstructing Paradise." Rev. of *Tehanu*. *Times Literary Supplement* 28 December 1990: 1409.

Barrow, Craig and Diana. "Le Guin's Earthsea: Voyages in Conciousness [*sic*]." *Extrapolation* 32 (1991): 20–44.

Jose, Jim. "Reflections on the Politics of Le Guin's Narrative Shifts." *Science-Fiction Studies* 18 (1991): 180–97.

Disch, Thomas M. "Big Ideas and Dead-End Thrills." *Atlantic* 269 (February 1992): 86–94.

Klarer, Mario. "Gender and the Simultaneity Principle: Ursula Le Guin's *The Dispossessed*." *Mosaic* 25 (Spring 1992): 107–121.

Barry, Nora, and Mary Prescott. "Beyond Words: The Impact of Rhythm as Narrative Technique in *The Left Hand of Darkness*." *Extrapolation* 33 (Summer 1992): 154–65.

Hatfield, Len. "From Master to Brother: Shifting the Balance of Authority in Ursula K. Le Guin's *Farthest Shore* and *Tehanu*." *Children's Literature* 21 (1993): 43–65.

Harper, Mary Catherine. "Spiraling around the Hinge: Working Solutions in *Always Coming Home*." *Old West-New West: Centennial Essays*. Ed. Barbara Howard Meldrum. Moscow: U of Idaho P, 1993. 241–57.

Barr, Marleen S. *Lost in Space: Probing Feminist Science Fiction and Beyond.* Chapel Hill: The U of North Carolina P, 1993.

Littlefield, Holly. "Unlearning Patriarchy: Ursula Le Guin's Feminist Consciousness in *The Tombs of Atuan* and *Tehanu.*" *Extrapolation* 16 (Fall 1995): 244–58.

Nodelman, Perry. "Reinventing the Past: Gender in Ursula K. Le Guin's *Tehanu* and the Earthsea 'Trilogy.'" *Children's Literature* 23 (1995): 179–201.

Murphy, Patrick D. *Literature, Nature, and Other: Ecofeminist Critiques.* Albany: State U of New York P, 1995.

Bratman, David S. *Ursula K. Le Guin: A Primary Bibliography.* Unpublished, 1995.

Lindow, Sandra. "Ursula K. Le Guin's Earthsea: Rescuing the Damaged Child." *New York Review of Science Fiction* 9.5 (January 1997): 1, 10–13.

Lindow, Sandra. "Trauma and Recovery in Ursula K. Le Guin's *Wonderful Alexander.* Animal as Guide Through the Inner Space of the Unconscious." *Foundation* 70 (Summer 1997): 32–38.

Donawerth, Jane. *Frankenstein's Daughters: Women Writing Science Fiction.* Syracuse: Syracuse UP, 1997.

Reid, Suzanne Elizabeth. Presenting Ursula K. Le Guin. Twayne's United States Authors Series 677. New York: Twayne Publishers, 1997.

Index

abused child, in works of Le Guin, 107, 110–11

Ace Books, 9, 44–45, 46

adventure, heroic. *See* romance, heroic

Aeneid, The (Virgil), 25, 38–39

Again, Dangerous Visions (Ellison), 51, 64

ageism. *See* old age, in works of Le Guin

Aldiss, Brian, 96

Alexander, Lloyd, 10, 27, 37

Algeo, John, 67–68

Algol, 16, 51

allegory, in works of Le Guin, 14, 16, 20, 24, 65–66, 83

Always Coming Home: attack on, 4, 96–97; as feminist utopia, 82, 95, 98–99, 102; imagery in, 99, 101–2; as political commentary, 97–98; reception of, 96–97, 116; structure of, 96, 98, 99, 100, 118; as utopian literature, 5, 46, 98, 100

Amazing, 9, 44, 64

Analog, 45

anarchism: in fictional background, 70, 83, 90; as form of sociology, 89–90; and language, 92–93; as stage in Le Guin's politics, 55–56; and Taoism, 89, 96; as theme, 117; and utopia, 87–88, 94

androgyny: in fiction, 46, 52, 59, 60; history of, 60; masculine aspects of, 47–49, 72–73

anthropologist, hero as, 55, 61, 70

anthropology: as background in Le Guin's life, 3, 11, 21, 63, 72, 118; as critical approach, 116,

117; in Earthsea books, 12, 21–23, 36, 39; and science fiction, 58–59, 62–63, 70, 75, 98, 102

Aphrodite, 28

apocalypse, 52, 53

"April in Paris," 44, 61, 62

archetypes, 36, 38, 39, 53, 109, 117; Anima/Animus, 30, 114; Child, 30; Self, 30, 31; Shadow, 12, 17, 28, 29, 30, 35, 114; Wise Old Man, 28, 30

archipelago, 10, 11, 12, 14

Ariadne, myth of, 14, 28, 33, 37

Aristotle, 61

Arthur, King, legend of, 38

artist, as creator, 16, 18, 20, 21

Astounding, 2, 9

Atheneum Books, 13, 64

Atlantic Monthly, 106

Attebery, Brian, 37–38, 113–14

Atwood, Margaret, 99; *Handmaid's Tale, The*, 99

Australian Science Fiction Review, 45

awards, literary: *Boston Globe-Horn Book*, 11, 15; Hugo, 1, 46, 54, 84; National Book Award, 1, 14, 15, 51, 83, 97; Nebula, 1, 14, 46, 54, 84, 107, 109; Newbery, 1, 11, 14

Babel-17 (Delany), 74

Bailey, Edgar C., Jr., 35

balance: of ends and means, 31; of life, 19, 20, 30; of opposites, 18, 30, 32, 39, 51–52, 55, 56, 110, 115, 117; structural, 36

balkanization, of Le Guin criticism, 2, 5, 23–24, 31–32